Visual Science
Encyclopedia

Electricity
and
Magnetism

▲ Electricity has been an invaluable aid in a wide range of activities, including lighting, heating and communications.

How to use this book

Every word defined in this book can be found in alphabetical order on pages 3 to 47. There is also a full index on page 48. A number of other features will help you get the most out of the *Visual Science Encyclopedia*. They are shown below.

Here you will find the first word defined on any left-hand page.

Each word is shown in bold so it is easy to find.

Other words defined in the book are highlighted in bold.

Plus, many entries point to related words of interest.

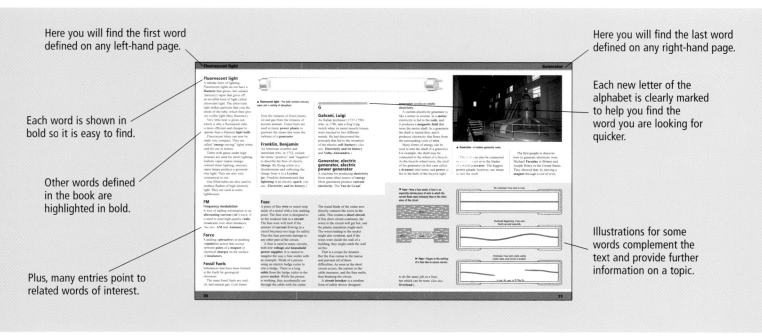

Here you will find the last word defined on any right-hand page.

Each new letter of the alphabet is clearly marked to help you find the word you are looking for quicker.

Illustrations for some words complement the text and provide further information on a topic.

First published in 2002 by Atlantic Europe Publishing Company Ltd

Copyright © 2002 Atlantic Europe Publishing Company Ltd

Author
Brian Knapp, BSc, PhD

Art Director
Duncan McCrae, BSc

Senior Designer
Adele Humphries, BA, PGCE

Editors
Lisa Magloff, BA, and
Mary Sanders, BSc

Illustrations
David Woodroffe

Designed and produced by
EARTHSCAPE EDITIONS

Reproduced in Malaysia by
Global Colour

Printed in Hong Kong by
Wing King Tong Company Ltd.

Visual Science Encyclopedia
Volume 8 *Electricity and magnetism*
A CIP record for this book is available from the British Library

ISBN 1-86214-034-0

Picture credits
All photographs are from the Earthscape Editions photolibrary.

This product is manufactured from sustainable managed forests. For every tree cut down, at least one more is planted.

A

AC

(*See:* **Alternating current**.)

Accumulator

A older term for a large **battery** (wet cell) that has lead plates and a liquid to conduct **electricity**. A car battery is a common example of an accumulator. (*See also:* **Secondary battery, cell** and **Telegraph**.)

Adapter

A device that makes it possible to use the same piece of electrical equipment in different countries.

An American **plug** and **socket** are not the same as those in Europe, Asia, or Australia, for example.

Also, the **power supply** is not the same in every country. If you go on holiday to another country and take an electrical device, you may not be able to plug it into the wall socket. That may be because the country you are visiting uses different-shaped plugs.

An adapter is a device that you put your plug into. The pins on the adapter then plug into the wall socket of the country you are visiting.

In some countries not only are the pins on the plugs different, but the **voltage** is also different. This is particularly true between North American countries and the rest of the world. In northern Europe the voltage is 240V, in Australasia it is also 240V, but in North America it is 120V. That means that an adapter on its own will not be enough. You need equipment that is designed to work on different voltages. Most computers and other electrical devices designed with the traveller in mind do this. If your equipment does not do this, then it is unsafe to use overseas.

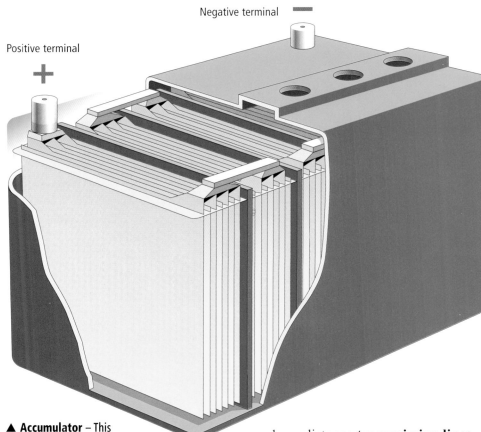

Positive terminal

Negative terminal

▲ **Accumulator** – This car battery is an accumulator. The plates are organised into cells, and each cell is divided from its neighbours. Conductors across the top of the accumulator connect the cells in series to produce 12V.

Aerial

(*See:* **Antenna**.)

Alkaline battery

A long-life **battery**. The life of a battery is partly controlled by size (the bigger the battery, the longer it lasts) and partly by the materials used to make it. An alkaline battery uses a special (alkaline) paste to ensure longer life and a more even **voltage** output throughout the battery's life.

Alternating current (AC)

A form of **electricity** in which the **current** changes direction regularly. The reason for making the current change rapidly is to allow the electricity supply to be carried most economically over long-distance **transmission lines**. This is done using high **voltages**. However, equipment in the home does not use high voltages. The voltage therefore has to be reduced by a piece of equipment called a **transformer**. Transformers only work with AC current. **Direct current (DC)** cannot be sent economically over long distances.

In most countries of the world the direction of the current alters 50 times a second. In North America it changes 60 times a second.

An AC or DC supply can be used by lights, stoves, and most home **appliances**. An AC supply cannot be used by computers, **radios**, and electronics and has to be converted to DC. Usually there is a special **circuit** inside the equipment to do this called a **rectifier**, but sometimes the rectifier is part of the **plug**.

AC circuits obey many of the same laws of electricity as DC circuits. For example, AC circuits obey **Ohm's Law**. (*See also:* **Tesla, Nikola**.)

AM
Amplitude modulated
A way of sending a **radio** signal. It is used for long-, medium-, and short-wave broadcasts. (*See also:* **Antenna** and **FM**.)

Ammeter
A **meter** for measuring electric **current**. It is often part of a **circuit tester** or multimeter. (*See also:* **Ohmmeter**.)

Amp (A)
The unit of electrical **current**.

Formally called the ampere, in honor of the French Scientist André **Ampere**, it is usually shortened to amp (A). The maximum current a **fuse** will take is written on the fuseholder in amps, for example, 5A, 10A.

Ampere, André Marie
A French professor and experimental scientist (1775–1836).

In the 1820s André Ampere showed that a coil of **wire** can act as a **magnet**. He was also responsible for designing an instrument to measure electric **current**. It is called a galvanometer. It consists of a coil of wire around a **magnetised** pointer that is allowed to turn freely. The stronger the current flowing, the more the pointer turns.

Amplify
To make something larger. Amplifiers are used to make weak electrical signals stronger. All **radios**, **televisions**, CD players, and similar equipment contain amplifiers in their **circuits**.

Antenna
A length of **wire** or metal rod that intercepts radio waves travelling through space and changes them into an electric **current** that can then be **amplified** to create pictures or sound or to operate equipment remotely.

The kind of antenna depends on the nature of the signal. In general, an antenna is either a fraction or a multiple of the wavelengths of the signal being transmitted. In the early days of **radio**, when transmitters sent out radio waves with a long wavelength (**AM**), a long wire was needed. **FM** radio works on shorter wavelengths, and so the length of antenna is shorter. **Television** works on even shorter wavelengths – called VHF (very high frequency) and UHF (ultra-high frequency).

Some antennas are in the form of wires strung between **utility poles**. Astronomical and transmitting antennas are sometimes like this.

▶ **Appliance**—This is a vacuum cleaner. It is a typical domestic electrical appliance. Other appliances include stoves and dishwashers.

Others are in the form of vertical rods (for example, the kind used in cars and mobile phones). Antennas also come in the form of horizontal bars (as used for home FM and TV) or they look like dishes. Dishes are only needed when the signal is weak or the wavelength very short, as in satellite TV broadcasts. In portable radios the antenna is wrapped around a bar of a special iron compound called ferrite. It helps magnify the signal and makes it possible to receive strong local broadcasts without an external antenna. (*See also:* **Coaxial cable**.)

Appliance
A piece of equipment that uses **electricity**, usually for a task around the home.

An appliance is a **power** device that is intended to apply electricity to do a labour-saving job. The word is mostly used for large appliances such as freezers and washing machines. Sometimes the term 'small appliance' is used for items like **irons** and **toasters**. (*See also:* **Plug, electrical**.)

▼ **Antenna** – This is a TV antenna. The receiving part of the antenna is the loop near the end. The rods and the plate are to help strengthen the signal. The plate behind the antenna is called a reflector.

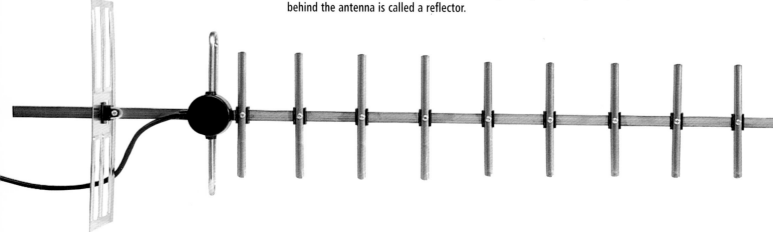

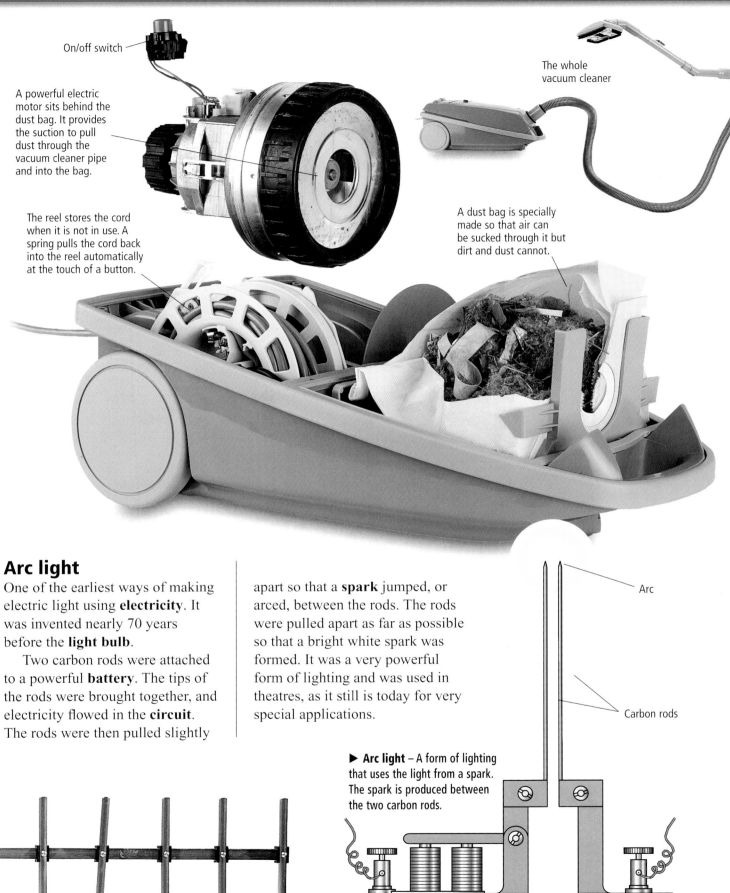

On/off switch

A powerful electric motor sits behind the dust bag. It provides the suction to pull dust through the vacuum cleaner pipe and into the bag.

The reel stores the cord when it is not in use. A spring pulls the cord back into the reel automatically at the touch of a button.

The whole vacuum cleaner

A dust bag is specially made so that air can be sucked through it but dirt and dust cannot.

Arc light

One of the earliest ways of making electric light using **electricity**. It was invented nearly 70 years before the **light bulb**.

Two carbon rods were attached to a powerful **battery**. The tips of the rods were brought together, and electricity flowed in the **circuit**. The rods were then pulled slightly apart so that a **spark** jumped, or arced, between the rods. The rods were pulled apart as far as possible so that a bright white spark was formed. It was a very powerful form of lighting and was used in theatres, as it still is today for very special applications.

▶ **Arc light** – A form of lighting that uses the light from a spark. The spark is produced between the two carbon rods.

Arc

Carbon rods

Armoured cable

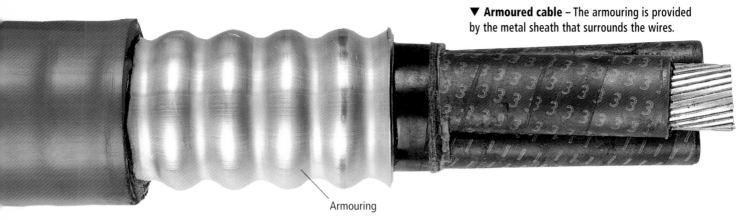

▼ **Armoured cable** – The armouring is provided by the metal sheath that surrounds the wires.

Armouring

Armoured cable

Electrical **wires** protected by metal sheathing. Armoured cables are used when a **cable** has to be buried, for example, when taking a **power supply** from a house to garden lighting, or when connecting the supply from the street to a house.

Attractive force

The **force** of attraction between opposites.

For example, the force that pulls together two opposite **poles** of a **magnet** (a **north pole** attracts a **south pole**) or two opposite **charges** in electricity (a positive charge attracts a negative charge in **static electricity**). (*Compare with:* **Repulsive force**.)

B

Battery

A device for turning chemical **energy** into **electrical energy**. A battery is also a way of carrying around a supply of **electricity**.

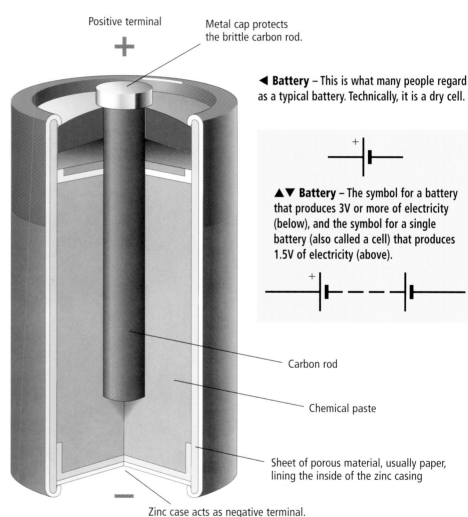

Positive terminal

Metal cap protects the brittle carbon rod.

◀ **Battery** – This is what many people regard as a typical battery. Technically, it is a dry cell.

▲▼ **Battery** – The symbol for a battery that produces 3V or more of electricity (below), and the symbol for a single battery (also called a cell) that produces 1.5V of electricity (above).

Carbon rod

Chemical paste

Sheet of porous material, usually paper, lining the inside of the zinc casing

Zinc case acts as negative terminal.

Battery type	Characteristics	Typical uses	Advantages and disadvantages
Lead–acid	Rechargeable	Car battery	Gives high output for turning starter motor, but bulky and heavy
Economy (zinc–carbon)	Voltage drops soon after use	Portable devices, bells, etc.	Low price, but short life
Alkaline	Constant voltage given out for most of its life	Used for portable radios, toys, etc.	More expensive than economy batteries, but longer life
Lithium	Constant voltage through its life	Used in watches, etc.	Stores the most energy for its size, lasts for years, expensive

The word battery is often used for any portable source of electricity. Strictly, a battery is a collection of **cells** stacked together in one case. The 1.5 **volt** (V) 'batteries' used in many pieces of equipment should properly be called 1.5V cells.

Dry cells that have chemical pastes inside usually have a value of 1.5V. A 9V battery contains six 1.5V dry cells stacked together end to end in a row (in series).

In a battery made of wet cells, sometimes called an **accumulator**, each cell produces 2V. Six cells are placed in line inside an accumulator to produce a 12V supply, as in car batteries.

Most dry batteries cannot be reused, although some batteries are **rechargeable**.

In a wet cell (accumulator) the metals are usually lead, and the liquid is usually sulphuric acid.

(*See also:* **Alkaline battery**; **Negative terminal**; **Positive terminal**; **Primary battery, cell**; **Secondary battery, cell**.)

History of batteries

When batteries were first invented, it was not easy to think of a use for them because most electric devices, such as **light bulbs**, had not yet been invented. The earliest use for batteries (in the 1830s) was in providing **power** for the **telegraph** system.

In the 1870s the electric door **bell** was invented. It became a fashionable device, and as a result the demand for batteries grew.

Light bulbs took longer to develop and were only generally on sale beginning in the early 1900s. Low-**voltage flashlight** bulbs were quickly developed. The first flashlights were sold as novelties, in part because the batteries were large, heavy and expensive. It took some years for lightweight batteries to be developed; and when they were, the flashlight came into general use.

▼ **Bell, electromagnetic** – The two diagrams below show how an electromagnetic bell works. When the switch is closed (left), the coils on the U-shaped iron core create a magnetic field that pulls the hammer onto the bell. The hammer, however, is part of the electrical circuit; and as the hammer moves, it breaks the circuit, and the coils lose their magnetism. As a result the hammer springs back to its resting position (right). As it reaches its rest position, the circuit is closed, bringing the hammer against the bell again. (Many modern door bells are electronic.)

Bell, electromagnetic

A device for converting **electricity** into a ringing sound. The bell is a good example of an **electromagnet** at work.

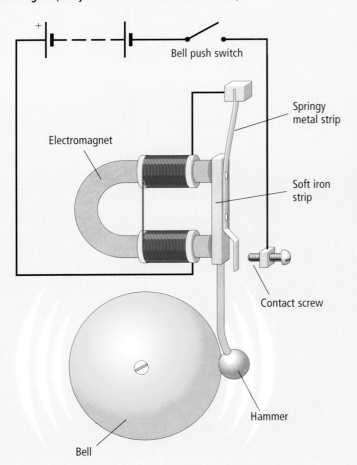

Bell push switch

Electromagnet

Springy metal strip

Soft iron strip

Contact screw

Hammer

Bell

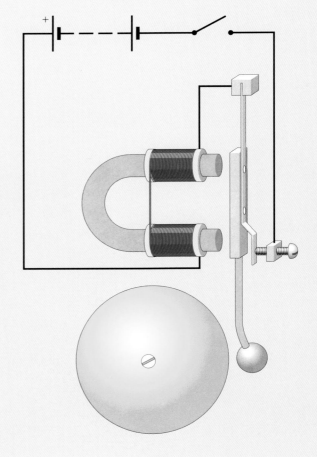

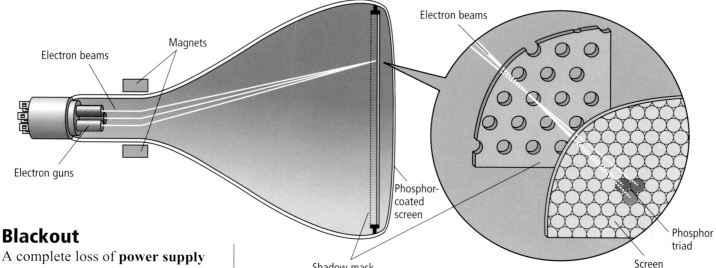

Electron beams

Magnets

Electron beams

Electron guns

Phosphor-coated screen

Shadow mask

Phosphor triad

Screen

Blackout

A complete loss of **power supply** due to an **overload**.

Brownout

A reduction in **voltage** that occurs when the electricity demand is greater than the **generators** can produce. Administrators in the utility company reduce the voltage to areas in rotation, cutting the **power supply** to all consumers.
(*See also:* **Overload**.)

Buzzer

A device for converting **electricity** into sound.

A buzzer contains a crystal that vibrates when electricity passes through it. It produces a relatively quiet buzzing sound. (*See also:* **Bell, electromagnetic**.)

C

Cable

The name used for a thick **wire**, for example, the cables that carry the **power supply** from **power stations** to homes. Cables are often made of strands of wire twisted together. (*See also:* **Armoured cable**; **Coaxial cable**; **Conductor**; **Electricity grid**.)

Capacitor

An electronic device that temporarily stores **electrical**

energy (as **static**). It is made from two conducting plates separated by an insulating material (*see:* **Conductor** and **Insulator**). The amount of electric **charge** stored depends on the surface area of the plates; so the bigger the plates, the more charge is stored.

To save space, most capacitors are rolled into a tube, with the insulating material sandwiched between the conducting plates (*see:* **Dielectric**). The standard unit of capacitance is the **farad**, abbreviated to F. Most capacitors used in electronic equipment are small and are measured in microfarads, abbreviated µF. (1µF equals one-millionth of a farad.)

Capacitors can be built into **integrated circuits** (chips). They are important **components** of most electronic equipment. In a computer they store charge temporarily and act as part of the computer memory.

Large capacitors are used with **rectifiers** to smooth out an AC (**alternating current**) supply and create the DC (**direct current**) supply needed for electronic equipment.

▲ **Cathode-ray tube** – The cathode-ray tube provides the picture for most TVs and computers.

Cathode-ray tube

A special form of **vacuum tube** with a long neck and a broad, flat screen on which images are produced. They are used for **televisions** and computer monitors.

In the neck of the cathode-ray tube is a source of **electrons** called an electron gun. It fires electrons at tiny phosphorescent dots on the screen, causing them to glow. Patterns of glowing dots make up pictures. In a colour tube there are three guns, firing beams that react on red, green and blue phosphors.

Along the neck of the tube are coils of **wire** that can be **magnetised** to control the exact direction in which the electrons strike the screen. They are used to make the electron gun scan the screen hundreds of times a second in a pattern similar to reading the lines on a page. That allows the picture to change quickly, giving the impression of movement on the screen.

◀ **Capacitor** – This is the kind of capacitor used in electronic circuits.

Note that cathode-ray screens cannot be used in portable computers; a different technology is used for them that involves liquid crystal displays (LCDs).

Cell

A portable supply of **electricity**.

A cell is a small chemical factory for producing electricity. It is the tubular '**battery**' you use in portable equipment. This form of cell is called a **dry cell**.

Strictly speaking, a battery is two or more cells placed end to end. The usual tubular versions of dry cells produce 1.5V of electricity. However, people commonly use the word battery for both cells and batteries.

(*For types of cell see:* **Photoelectric cell**; **Photovoltaic cell**; **Primary battery, cell**; **Rechargeable battery, cell**; **Secondary battery, cell**.)

Charge

The build-up of **electricity**.

People use the word charge in two ways. Firstly, when talking about **static electricity**. A surface of an **insulator** can have a positive charge or a negative charge. When two substances rub together, the positive charges can be rubbed off onto one surface and the negative ones onto the other. Each surface now has an opposite charge and so they will attract each other (*see:* **Attractive force**). Sometimes the charges will jump the gap and then a **spark** will occur.

Secondly, charge can also be used in terms of charging up a **battery**, meaning to cause a **rechargeable battery** to reach its full storage of electricity.

(*See also:* **Coulomb (C)**.)

Chip

(*See:* **Silicon chip**.)

Circuit

A continuous path for the flow of **electricity**. It contains a collection of electrical **components** and connections.

All circuits must have three parts:

- A source of **power** (for example, a **battery**);
- **Wires** to connect the pieces of the circuit;
- A **light bulb**, a **buzzer**, or something else (called a **load**) that works on electricity.

Most circuits also have:

- A **switch** for controlling the flow of electricity.

Circuits can be very complicated, but essentially all circuits are made of just two patterns called **series circuits** and **parallel circuits**. In a series circuit each of the components is connected to the **power supply** in a single, continuous loop. In a parallel circuit the components are connected side by side, so that they are, in effect, each connected directly to the power supply. In this case, if the flow of electricity to one component is cut off by a switch, that does not affect the flow to the others and they keep working. Most circuits in the home are parallel circuits. Most circuits in electronic equipment are a combination of series and parallel circuits.

(*See also:* **Circuit board**; **Circuit breaker**; **Circuit diagram**; **Conductor**; **Fuse**; **Integrated circuit**; **Resistor**; **Semi-conductor**.)

How a circuit works

To understand how a circuit works, think of the power supply as a water pump driving a fountain in a pond. The fountain is like a light bulb or like anything else we want to make work. It is the load.

▼ **Circuit** – This is the simplest form of a circuit, with a power source (the batteries) and a load (the bulb).

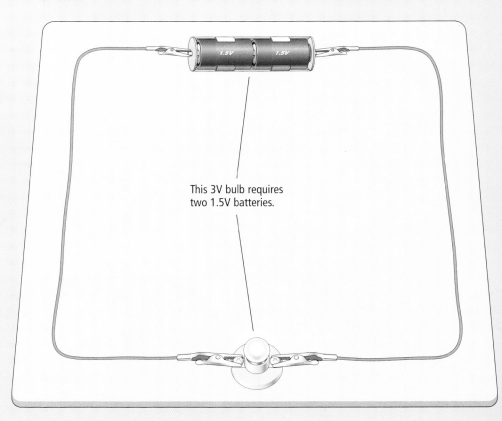

This 3V bulb requires two 1.5V batteries.

The water pump can only pump water through the fountain if the fountain water falls back in the pond so that it can be sucked up again. The battery can only make the load work if it is connected to the load in a loop so that the electricity used to make the load work can return to the battery.

Eventually, the water in the pond evaporates and the pump stops. That is equivalent to the battery being used up.

Any wire connected across the terminals of the battery makes a circuit for electricity to flow. If a single wire were connected across the battery, it would make a special kind of circuit called a **short circuit**. The wire would get very hot and the battery would rapidly be used up.

A switch breaks the circuit, controlling the electricity flow.

Problems with circuits

If a circuit does nothing, it may be because:
- The battery is used up, the load has a broken wire inside it, or the connecting wires have a break somewhere;
- The wires do not make a loop that includes both the load and the battery.

Faulty circuits are not always easy to spot. Bad connections can happen when two wires are connected without first taking off the insulation, or when one wire is wrapped around the insulation of the other. (*See also:* **Circuit tester** and **Meter**.)

▶ **Circuit board** – This is part of the underside of a circuit board, showing the printed circuit made of copper strip. The components are pushed through holes in the board and soldered to the copper. The solder shows as silvery blobs.

Circuit board

A device containing **circuit** connectors.

A circuit board is made out of an insulating material such as plastic. Instead of using **wires**, strips of metal are stuck to the board.

Holes are drilled through the board to match the **components** that are to be connected. The wires, or connectors, from the components are then pushed through the holes in the board and soldered to the metal strips.

Using a circuit board in this way produces a very reliable circuit with connections that are easy to check.

Circuit breaker

A form of **fuse** that can be reused. It is designed to break the electrical **circuit** if there is a chance of **overload**. It works by **electromagnetism**. A **coil** inside the circuit breaker creates an **electromagnet**. The more

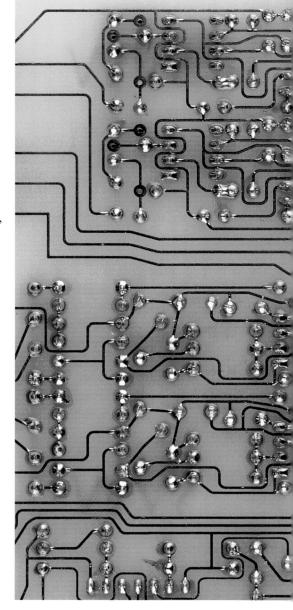

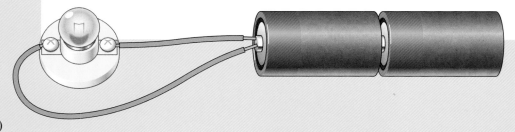

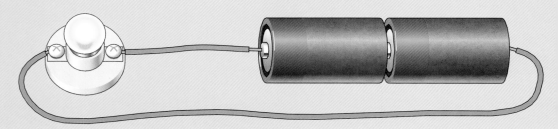

▶ **Circuit** – The top diagram shows an incorrectly wired circuit. No loop is formed from one battery terminal to the other and so no electricity flows. The lower diagram shows the correct wiring.

10

the **current** flows, the stronger the electromagnet becomes. If the current gets very large, the electromagnetic force becomes powerful enough to pull a **switch** and break the circuit.

The advantage of a circuit breaker over a fuse is that the switch can be reset after the fault that caused the overload has been located. A fuse would have to be replaced.

Circuit diagram

A drawing that shows the arrangement of electrical **components** and **wires** in a **circuit** by using **symbols**. It is an electrician's map.

Circuit diagrams always show three things:

- A source of **power** (for example, a **battery**);
- The wires that connect the pieces of the circuit;
- A **light bulb**, a **buzzer**, or something else that works on electricity. It is called the **load**.

The circuit diagram is very useful because it can be read by everyone. That is because it uses a set of agreed-on symbols like colours or shapes on any map. This gets around the problem of manufacturers making differently shaped components.

There are some important rules to be followed when drawing circuit diagrams:

- The wires must always connect the components;
- The wires must always be in straight lines;
- When wires change direction, it is always at right angles.

When you make a circuit using a circuit diagram, you can make the circuit look like the diagram, or you can place the wires and components wherever you want. The only important thing is that they are linked up in the same pattern as on the diagram. (*See also:* **Series circuit**.)

Circuit tester

A **meter** designed to allow electricians to find out the **voltage** and **current** flowing in a **circuit**. Most also measure the **resistance** of **components**. (*See also:* **Ammeter**; **Ohmmeter**; **Voltmeter**.)

Coaxial cable

A **cable** used to connect **antennas** to **televisions** and hi-fi equipment. A coaxial cable consists of a central core of solid copper, surrounded by a plastic sleeve, which is in turn enclosed by a sheath of braided copper **wires** and another plastic sleeve. The central wire carries the signal, while the outer sheath acts as a ground and shields the signal cable from interference.

Coil

A length of **wire** wound around a tube. It is used to make an **electromagnet** and other electronic **components**. Tuning coils used inside **radio** and **television** equipment detect incoming signals. **Transformers** are paired coils on the same iron core. (*See also:* **Solenoid**.)

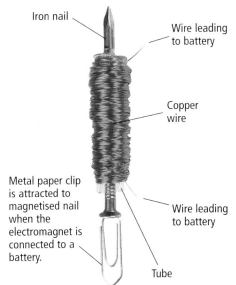

▼ **Coil** – This coil can be used to make an electromagnet.

Iron nail

Wire leading to battery

Copper wire

Metal paper clip is attracted to magnetised nail when the electromagnet is connected to a battery.

Wire leading to battery

Tube

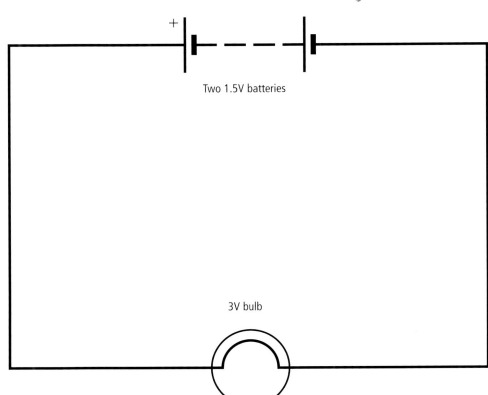

+

Two 1.5V batteries

3V bulb

▶ **Circuit diagram** – This is a circuit diagram for the circuit on page 9.

Compass

A **magnetised** needle that can move freely on a pointed pivot. A compass will:

- Naturally point towards the Earth's magnetic north pole;
- Change angle when a magnetic material is brought near;
- Change angle when placed close to a **wire** carrying an electric **current**.

When **electricity** flows through a wire, the wire develops a **magnetic field**. A compass placed close to a wire with an electric **current** flowing through it will change to face the **north pole** of the wire.

If a current is passed through a meter of insulated wire wrapped around a compass, the magnetic effect will be much more pronounced because the wire has been made into a **coil**. The compass now indicates when current is flowing through the wire. This is the simplest kind of **meter**.

(*See also:* **Magnet**.)

Component

One of the parts of an electric **circuit**.

Buzzers, **light bulbs** and similar devices are components. **Batteries** and **wires** are not components; batteries are sources of **power** and wires are connectors between components.

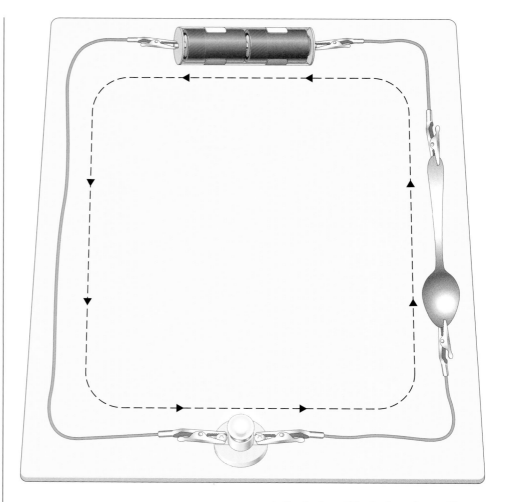

Conductor

Any material that will allow **electricity** to pass freely through it. Materials that do not allow the flow of electricity are called **insulators**. (*See also:* **Semi-conductors**.)

The flow of electricity through a conductor is called electric **current**. The current is measured in a unit called **amps**.

Most metals are conductors. Metals are the most widely used conductors because they can be bent into shapes or made into thin, flexible **wires**.

◄ **Components** – A selection of components. From right to left: diode, paper capacitor, three resistors, an electrolytic capacitor.

▲ **Conductor** – This circuit can be used for testing a conductor by simply replacing the spoon with another object. If the object is a conductor, the bulb will light, and a current (shown by the dashed line) will flow.

Carbon is the most important non-metallic conductor. Carbon is used as a conductor in **dry cells** and **motors**. But it is too soft and brittle to be used directly in **circuits**.

Some materials conduct electricity very easily. Silver and gold are the best conductors, but they are too expensive for everyday uses, and silver also tarnishes quickly (the tarnish is silver sulphide, an insulator). Copper is the best conductor among cheaper metals, and it will bend many times without breaking. It is also soft and pliable. For these reasons copper is often used for the connecting wires in circuits. Aluminium is also a good conductor. It is lighter and even cheaper than copper, so it is used for long-distance **cables**. It is not as pliable as copper and is not used in home circuits.

Other metals conduct electricity less easily. That is, they resist the flow of current (they are **resistors**). This can be a useful property, especially in the case of metals with high melting points. Two important resistors are tungsten, used for the **filaments** in **light bulbs** and nichrome, a mixture of the metals chromium and nickel, used for the **elements** in heaters.

(*See also:* **Electrolyte**.)

Contacts

Flat metal blades of a **switch**, the pins on a **plug**, or the pins or screw fitting of a **light bulb**.

Contacts are designed to make a good connection in a switch, plug, or bulb. They also have to stand up to the **spark** that occurs each time the contacts close or open.

Contacts are often made of a material that remains bright and clean, such as brass (which is used for plugs). The contacts in plugs

The case makes one contact.

The shiny tip makes the other contact.

▲ **Contacts – These are the contacts on a flashlight bulb.**

on the ends of computer **cables** are coated with gold to make sure they always provide a good contact.

Coulomb (C)

The unit of electric **charge**.

Current

The amount of flow of **electricity** through a **circuit**. Electric current is measured in **amps (A)**.

An electric current can be compared with the way in which water flows in a river. Imagine the channel of the river as being like a **wire** and the flow of water through it like the current flowing through the wire. The bigger the river channel (or wire), the more water (or current) can flow.

The way current and **voltage** are related is explained by **Ohm's Law**.

There are two types of current: **direct current (DC)**, which was the first type of **current electricity** ever used and is still needed for electronic circuits, and **alternating current (AC)**, which is used for most **power supplies**.

AC is used for carrying electricity economically over long distances. In electronic circuits there is a special device, called a **transformer**, that steps down the **household power supply** into the low voltage needed for use by electronics. Another device, called a **rectifier**, is used to convert AC into DC. Some simple circuits, such as **light bulbs**, **motors** and heaters, can use AC directly. Motors that run on AC are also much more reliable than those that run on DC because they have a simpler design.

An electric current always produces a **magnetic field**. The stronger the current, the more intense the magnetic field. This field spreads out from the place it is made (the transmitter) and can produce a current in wires

elsewhere (the receiver). That is the principle of **television** and **radio** transmission and receiving. (*See also:* **Conductor** and **Semiconductor**.)

Current electricity

One of the two forms of **electricity**. Current electricity is the flow of **electrons** through **conductors**. (*See also:* **Static electricity**.)

D

DC

(*See:* **Direct current**.)

Dielectric

An **insulator** placed between two conducting plates in a **capacitor**. Paper, air and plastic are common dielectric materials.

Dimmer switch

A **switch** containing a **variable resistor**. As the knob on the dimmer is turned, the amount of **resistance** in the **circuit** decreases, and this increases the flowing **current**. With more current, a bulb shines more brightly. Dimmers will only work with **incandescent light bulbs**, not with **fluorescent** tubes.

Diode

A device that allows **electricity** to flow through it in only one direction. It is also known as a **rectifier**. Diodes are mostly made with **semi-conductors**.

Semi-conductor diodes can also be designed to produce **direct current** when visible light, infra-red, or ultra-violet light strikes them. These diodes are called **photovoltaic cells**, solar cells and photosensors. Diodes that emit light when a **current** passes through them are called LEDs (**Light-emitting diodes**).

Direct current (DC)

The continuous flow of **current** in one direction. Direct current is produced by a **dry cell** or **battery**. All electronic **circuits** use DC. The current produced by **power** companies is **alternating current (AC)**. To convert AC to DC requires a **rectifier**, usually a **diode**.

Dry cell

A device that turns chemicals into **electricity**. It is more commonly called a **battery**. Technically speaking, a battery is a collection of **cells** placed end to end.

A dry cell is used as a portable supply of electricity. The word 'dry' means that there is a paste inside the case, and not a liquid. This reduces the chance of accidental leakage if a cell is dropped or damaged. Dry cells are therefore safer than 'wet' cells.

In an economy dry cell, carbon, zinc and a chemical paste are used. The carbon is in the shape of a rod and is placed in the centre of the cell (*see also:* **Conductor**). The zinc is used for the metal case. The paste and a porous separating paper make up the rest of the cell.

The combination of materials used to make a dry cell determines the **voltage** of the cell. For most cells the voltage produced is 1.5V. That is why the rod-shaped dry cells (batteries) that you buy in the store have 1.5V printed on them.

Big cells last longer than small cells because they have a larger volume of chemicals inside. However, the size does not affect the voltage. A battery with 3V, 4.5V, 9V and so on, marked on the side is made of several dry cells placed end to end and hidden inside a case. (*See also:* **Direct current**; **Negative terminal**; **Positive terminal**.)

Dynamo

A small **generator** used to provide **electricity**.

(*See also:* **Electromagnet**.)

▼ **Dynamo** – This is a bicycle dynamo that has been cut open to show how the dynamo wheel (top), which is driven by the bicycle wheel, is connected to a tiny generator.

Direction of spin

This part is turned against the bicycle wheel.

Shaft

As the shaft turns, it moves a coil surrounded by magnets, and electricity is produced. It can power a bicycle light.

Wires go to bulbs.

E

Earth

(*See:* **Ground**.)

Edison, Thomas Alva

One of the pioneers of the practical application of **electricity**. Edison (1847–1931) was not a scientist, but an engineer. Among many other developments and inventions, he was responsible for a reliable **incandescent light bulb** and for a method for supplying **electric power** to neighbourhoods.

Edison linked together the manufacture of a reliable light bulb with the supply of electric lighting through the use of **power stations**. In this way he designed a complete lighting system that had a practical application. He did more than anyone else to make electric power usable in homes and factories.

Edison first tried out his power system in January 1882 in London, but the first commercial power station was on Pearl Street, New York City. It had just 85 customers and lit only 400 lamps.

Edison's system used **direct current**, which could not be transported very far. When Nikola **Tesla** invented **alternating current**, Edison opposed its adoption, but he was finally forced to accept its use, and then his power companies prospered.

Edison also discovered the principle of the **vacuum tube**, but he did not see a way to develop it. That was accomplished later by J. A. Fleming.

(*See also:* **Electricity and its history**.)

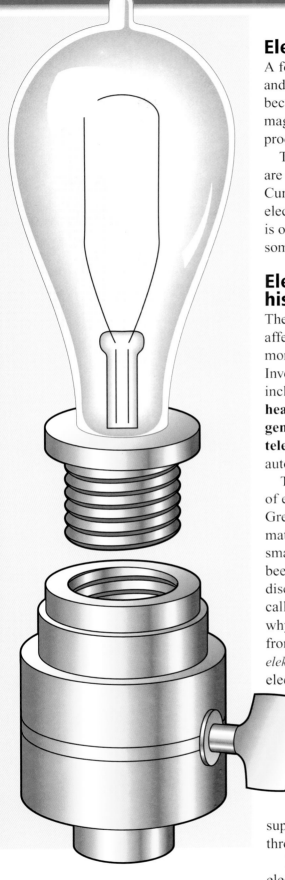

Electrical energy
The amount of electrical **power** produced per second. (*See also:* **Electricity**.)

Electricity
A form of **energy**. Electricity and **magnetism** are inseparable because electricity produces magnetism, and magnetism produces electricity.

The two forms of electricity are **current electricity** and **static**. Current electricity is used in all electrical **circuits**. Static electricity is only used for photocopiers and some other devices.

Electricity and its history
The discovery of **electricity** has affected our modern world perhaps more than any other innovation. Inventions that use electricity include electric lighting, electric **heating**, computers, **motors**, **generators**, telephones, **radio** and **television**, and the **circuits** that run automobiles.

The first people to become aware of electricity were the Ancient Greeks. They found that a natural material called amber attracted a small piece of fur after it had been rubbed by a cloth. They had discovered the form of electricity called **static electricity**. That is why the word electricity comes from the Greek word for amber, *elektron*. In fact, we now know that electricity is the transfer of small particles called **electrons**.

The British chemist Stephen Gray discovered in 1729 that electricity can flow. He sent **current electricity** 150 metres through a hemp thread supported by silk cords and also through metal **wire**.

In 1745 a way of storing electrical **charge** temporarily was invented by Pieter van Musschenbroek in Leyden, Netherlands. It was known as the **Leyden jar**. The principle was later used to develop the electronic **component** called the **capacitor**.

In 1747 William Watson, in Britain, transmitted an electric **spark** from a Leyden jar through a wire strung across the Thames at Westminster Bridge. Benjamin **Franklin**, in America, also experimented with sending electricity from one body to another. In 1752 Franklin demonstrated in a very dangerous experiment that **lightning** was an example of electricity. He flew a silk kite during a thunderstorm and collected electric charge from the cloud through wet twine attached to a key and a Leyden jar. It was Franklin who first termed an excess of electrical charge 'positive' and a lack of charge 'negative'. He believed that electricity flowed from positive to negative. In fact we now know that electrons flow the other way, although for the sake of history, the so-called 'conventional current' is still taken from positive to negative.

In the 18th century an assistant to the Italian scientist Luigi **Galvani** noticed that a dissected frog's leg twitched when he touched its nerve with a metal scalpel. Experimenting further, Galvani found that a frog's muscle would also twitch when hung by a brass hook on an iron railing. Another Italian scientist, Alessandro **Volta** (for whom the word **voltage** is named), showed that, when two metals are connected by some kinds of liquid, a flow of electricity results. By 1800, Volta had invented the electric **cell** (and **battery**).

An electric cell separates electrons by chemical means (rather than by rubbing, as is the case with static electricity). If the separated electrons are then removed, the battery will separate more electrons, thus changing chemical **energy** into **electrical energy**. That is current electricity.

Once a steady current of electricity could be produced from a battery, the German physicist Georg Simon **Ohm** was able to investigate the way that materials conducted electricity. As a result, he produced **Ohm's Law**.

In 1820 **Hans Christian Ørsted** demonstrated that electric currents produce magnetic effects. Michael **Faraday** then showed that a **magnet** could produce electricity. He laid the foundation for the electric motor and radio.

After this people tried to make use of electricity. Foremost in this was Thomas **Edison**, who was one of the first to develop electric light.

During the 20th century more and more attention was given to the use of **electromagnetism**, first to develop radio and then television. One of the most important inventions in this period was the **vacuum tube**. Then, in the middle of the 20th century William **Shockley** discovered how to make the **transistor**, and led the way to the miniature, low-**power** electronics that we use today in everything from computers to automobiles.

(*See also:* **Ampere, André Marie**; **Arc light**.)

Electricity grid, power grid, utility grid

A network of **cables** or **transmission lines** designed to connect **power stations** with their customers in offices, homes, schools and factories.

The cables are often carried on tall overhead **pylons** across the countryside, but in cities they run on **utility poles** or are buried underground.

(*See also:* **Substation**.)

Electric power

A term used in a general way to indicate a supply of **electricity** at high **voltage** – **household** voltage or above. Other terms include **power supply** or simply **power**. It is different from the more technical definition given by physicists to the word power.

Electric shock

A flow of **electricity** through the nerves of the human body as a result of contact with a powerful source of electricity. Because nerves send messages around the body using tiny electrical signals, the body is very sensitive to other forms of electricity. Handling low-voltage batteries cannot cause harm, but a flow of electricity through the body from a **household power supply**, or a flash of **lightning**, can damage the heart and brain, and even cause death.

Electrolysis

A method for passing **electricity** through a liquid to separate materials in the liquid.

Water, for example, can be split into hydrogen and oxygen by an electric **current**, as the following laboratory demonstration (and the picture on the right) shows. Electricity is an important source of **energy** for many chemical reactions. Pure water, however, is not a good **electrolyte** and has to be made more conductive by adding a small amount of a chemical like sodium sulphate.

Two platinum (non-reacting) electrodes are used to connect the **power supply** to the U-shaped tube in which the electrolysis occurs.

As the electric current is applied to the solution, gas is given off

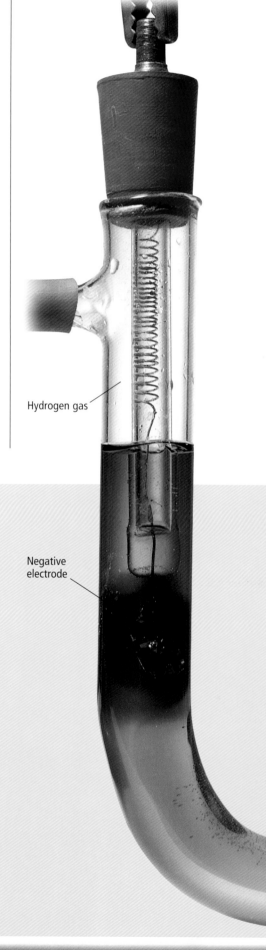

Hydrogen gas

Negative electrode

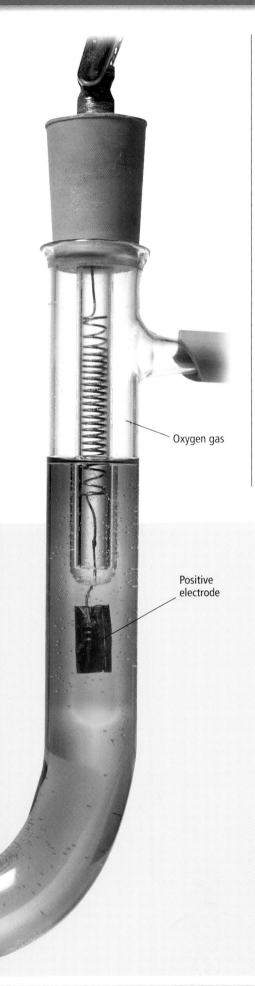

Oxygen gas

Positive electrode

Electrolyte

A liquid (or a paste) that conducts **electricity**. Tap water is an electrolyte, which is why it is unsafe to touch electricity with wet hands. (*See also:* **Electrolysis** and **Electroplating**.)

Electromagnet

A **magnet** produced by wrapping a **coil** around an iron rod and then passing **electricity** through the coil.

An electromagnet is a controllable temporary magnet. The magnetic effect can be made stronger by coiling more and more **wire** around the iron rod.

An electromagnet works as a very simple **circuit**. The source of **power** may be a **battery** and the **load** is the coil of wire. A **switch** can also be connected into the circuit to turn the **magnetic field** on and off.

◀ **Electrolysis – The splitting of water.**

at the electrodes. Hydrogen is liberated at the **negative terminal** (the one on the left in this picture), and oxygen is liberated at the positive terminal (on the right). This leaves an excess of hydrogen in the water on the right. A chemical indicator in the water changes colour to red to show the more acid conditions on the left. At the same time, more alkaline conditions develop on the right, and the indicator shows this by turning violet.

This process of electrolysis is widely used on an industrial scale, but with different apparatus.

(*See also:* **Electroplating**.)

An electromagnet behaves like a bar magnet. In an electromagnet the side of the coil attached to the **negative terminal** of the battery becomes the **north pole**, and the side attached to the **positive terminal** becomes the **south pole**.

Most magnets in use are electromagnets. There are electromagnets in all **motors** (like those in cassette players, washing machines, electric drills and so on). There are also electromagnets in the earpiece of a traditional telephone. The signal to the telephone is an electric **current**. As it changes in strength, a small electromagnet attracts and releases a thin steel plate. It is the vibration of this plate that makes the sound waves we hear.

Very powerful electromagnets are used to pick up and move iron and steel in scrap-yards.

Electromagnets are also used in electric **generators** in the central part of a **power station**. In this case a coil of wire is moved through the magnetic field of a magnet. It causes a current to flow in the wire, which is the current that eventually gets to your home.

Electromagnets with moving cores are also used to open and close **contacts**. When used in this way, electromagnets can work electric **bells** and switch on equipment by remote control. Every time a car is started, an electromagnet is used to make the starter motor work. Electromagnets with this type of moving core are called **solenoids**.

(*See also:* **Induction**.)

Electromagnetic field

The **magnetic field** produced when a **current** flows through a **wire**. (*See also:* **Electromagnet** and **Solenoid**.)

Electron

Negatively **charged** particles that flow in **wires** and other kinds of **conductors**, and produce an electric **current**. They flow from negative to positive. However, this was only understood relatively recently. For many years it had been assumed that the flow of electricity was from positive to negative. As a result, that is still how current is described. The traditional direction of current is known as the 'conventional current'. (*See also:* **Electricity and its history**.)

Electroplating

A way of using an electrical **current** to coat an object with metal. (*See also:* **Electrolysis** and **Electrolyte**.)

Element, electrical

In **electricity** an element is a **heating wire**.

The heating element can be left exposed and can provide heat directly to the air, as in a bar fire, or it can be enclosed, for example, if it is to be used under water in an **immersion heater**. A hair dryer also contains an element. The fan in the back of the dryer pushes air past the element and the air is warmed. Fires, **stoves**, **toasters** and many other **appliances** that produce heat all contain heating elements.

Energy

The ability to make something happen. **Electrical energy** makes lights shine, **bells** ring and so on.

F

Farad (F)

The unit of capacitance (*see:* **Capacitor**).

Faraday, Michael

One of the world's most important experimental scientists, Faraday (1791–1867) worked in the British Royal Institution. He built the world's first electric **motor** in 1821. He also found that a **current** flowing in one **wire** will cause a current to flow in another wire placed close by. That led to the discovery of the **transformer**.

Faraday was interested in lines of **magnetic** force. He was the first person to see lines of force of a **magnet** by scattering iron filings on a card placed on top of a magnet. (*See also:* **Electricity and its history** and **Generator**.)

Filament

The tightly coiled **wire** inside an electric **light bulb**.

A filament is made of a metal, such as tungsten, that gives some **resistance** to the flow of

▼▶ **Filament** – The filament of a light bulb and a section enlarged so that the curled nature of the wire can be seen.

electricity, and that has a high melting point. When an electric **current** flows through it, the wire heats up and gives out light.

Flashlight

A hand-held, electrical device for shining light.

A flashlight gives out light so that you can see in the dark. Flashlights use **batteries** and a very simple **circuit** with a bulb and a **switch**. When the flashlight is switched on, the **current** flows through the **filament** in the bulb. A reflector placed behind the bulb, and sometimes also a lens in front of it, bounce light forwards to produce a thin beam.

(*See also:* **Contacts**.)

Flex

A pair of insulated **wires** twisted together. Two-wire flex is normally used only for lights.

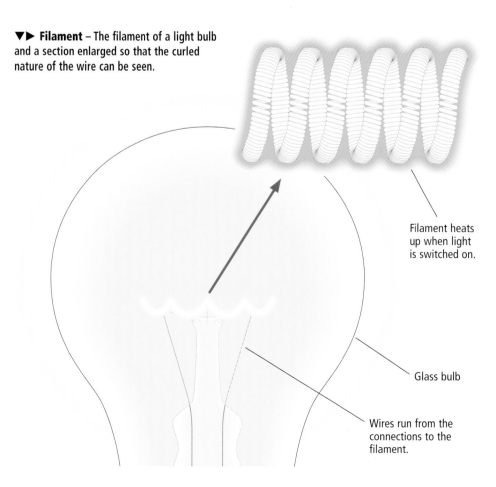

Filament heats up when light is switched on.

Glass bulb

Wires run from the connections to the filament.

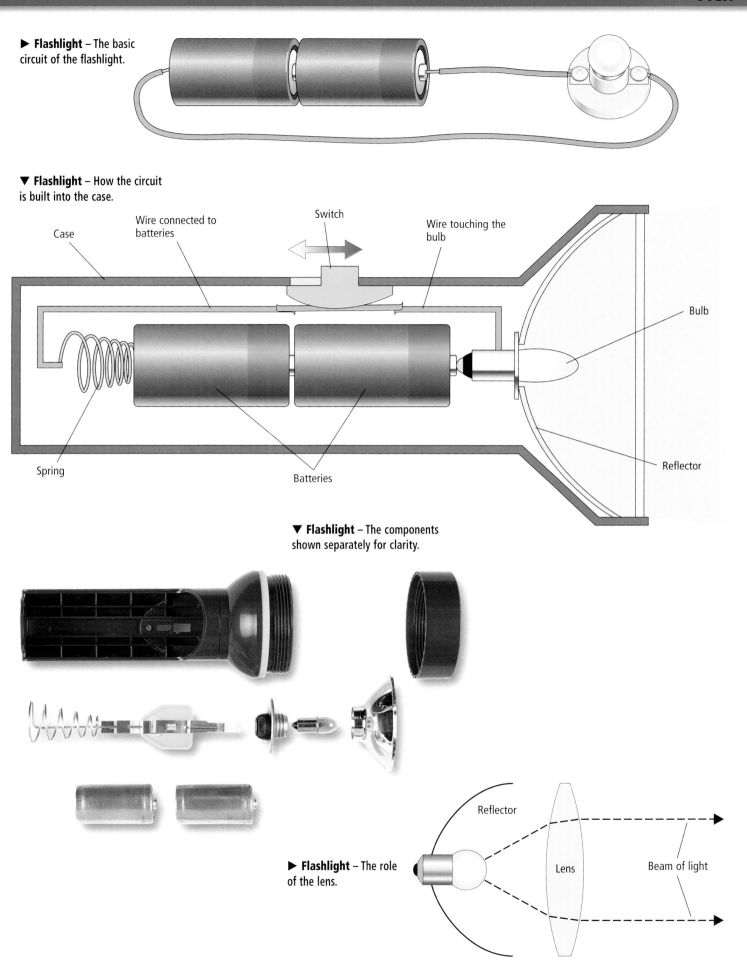

▶ **Flashlight** – The basic circuit of the flashlight.

▼ **Flashlight** – How the circuit is built into the case.

Case

Wire connected to batteries

Switch

Wire touching the bulb

Bulb

Spring

Batteries

Reflector

▼ **Flashlight** – The components shown separately for clarity.

▶ **Flashlight** – The role of the lens.

Reflector

Lens

Beam of light

Fluorescent light

A tubular form of lighting. Fluorescent lights do not have a **filament** that glows, but contain (mercury) vapour that gives off an invisible kind of light called ultra-violet light. The ultra-violet light strikes particles that coat the inside of the tube, which then give out visible light (they fluoresce).

Very little heat is given out, which is why a fluorescent tube is more efficient and cheaper to operate than a filament **light bulb**.

Fluorescent tubes can now be made very compact. They are called 'energy-saving' lights when sold for use in homes.

Tubes with gases under high pressure are used for street lighting. Sodium vapour makes orange-coloured street lighting; mercury vapour lamps produce a greenish-blue light. They are also very economical to run.

Gas-filled tubes are also used to produce flashes of high intensity light. They are used in some lighthouses.

▲ **Fluorescent light** – The bulb contains mercury vapour and a coating of phosphors.

FM

Frequency modulation

A way of adding information to an **alternating current (AC)** wave. It is used to send high-quality **radio** broadcasts over short distances. (*See also:* **AM** and **Antenna**.)

Force

A pulling (**attractive**) or pushing (**repulsive**) action that occurs between **poles** of a **magnet** or electrical **charges** on the surface of **insulators**.

Fossil fuels

Substances that have been formed in the Earth by geological processes.

The main fossil fuels are coal, oil and natural gas. Coal forms from the remains of fossil plants, oil and gas from the remains of ancient animals. Fossil fuels are used in many **power stations** to generate the steam that turns the turbines of a **generator**.

Franklin, Benjamin

An American scientist and statesman who, in 1752, coined the terms 'positive' and 'negative' to describe the flow of electric **charge**. By flying a kite in a thunderstorm and collecting the charge from it in a **Leyden jar**, Franklin demonstrated that **lightning** is an electric **spark**. (*See also:* **Electricity and its history**.)

Fuse

A piece of fine **wire** or metal strip made of a metal with a low melting point. The fuse wire is designed to be the weakest link in a **circuit**. The fuse wire will melt if the amount of **current** flowing in a circuit becomes too large for safety. Thus the fuse prevents damage to any other part of the circuit.

A fuse is used in many circuits, both low **voltage** and **household power supplies**. It is easiest to imagine the way in which a fuse works with an example. Think of a person using an electric hedge cutter to trim a hedge. There is a long **cable** from the hedge cutter to the power **socket**. While the person is working, they accidentally cut through the cable with the cutter.

G

Galvani, Luigi

An Italian professor (1737–1798) who, in 1786, saw a frog's leg twitch when its moist muscle tissues were in contact with two different metals. He had discovered the principle that led to the invention of the electric **cell** (**battery**). (*See also:* **Electricity and its history** and **Volta, Alessandro**.)

Generator, electric generator, electric power generator

A machine for producing **electricity** from some other source of **energy**. Most generators produce **current electricity**. The **Van de Graaf**

The metal blade of the cutter is now in direct contact with the wires in the cable. This creates a **short circuit**. If this short circuit continues, the wires in the circuit will get hot, and the plastic insulation might melt. The wires leading to the socket might also overheat; and if the wires were inside the wall of a building, they might catch the wall on fire.

That is a recipe for disaster. But the fuse comes to the rescue and prevents all of these difficulties. As soon as the short circuit occurs, the current in the cable increases, and the fuse melts, thus breaking the circuit.

A **circuit breaker** is a modern form of safety device designed

generator produces **static electricity**.

A current-electricity generator is like a motor in reverse. In a **motor** electricity is fed to the **coils**, and it produces a **magnetic field** that turns the motor shaft. In a generator the shaft is turned first, and it produces electricity that flows from the surrounding coils of **wire**.

Many forms of energy can be used to turn the shaft of a generator. For example, the shaft may be connected to the wheel of a bicycle. As the bicycle wheel turns, the shaft of the generator (in this case called a **dynamo**) also turns, and **power** is fed to the bulb of the bicycle light.

▲ **Generator** – A modern generator room.

The shaft can also be connected to a waterwheel or to the blades of a **wind generator**. The biggest **power stations**, however, use steam to turn the shaft.

The first people to discover how to generate electricity were Michael **Faraday** in Britain and Joseph Henry in the United States. They showed that, by moving a **magnet** through a coil of wire,

▼ **Fuse** – How a fuse works. A fuse is an especially narrow piece of wire in which the current flows more intensely than in the other wires of the circuit.

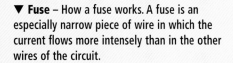

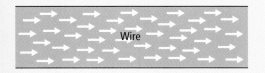

▶ **Fuse** – Stages in the melting of a fuse due to excess current.

to do the same job as a fuse, but which can be reset. (*See also:* **Overload**.)

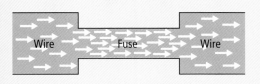

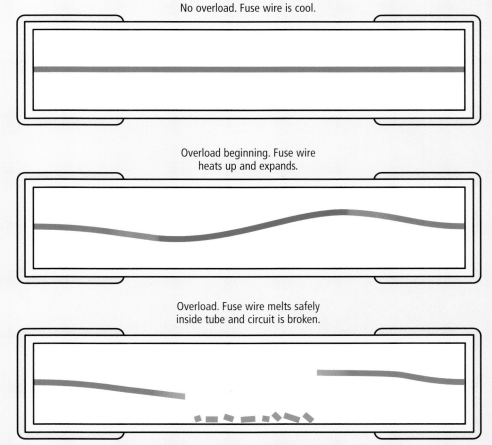

No overload. Fuse wire is cool.

Overload beginning. Fuse wire heats up and expands.

Overload. Fuse wire melts safely inside tube and circuit is broken.

electricity could be produced, or generated, in the wire.

Modern generators spin an **electromagnet** on a shaft inside huge coils of wire.

The **current** and the **voltage** of the electricity produced depend on the speed the shaft turns and on the strength of the magnetic field.

The generators used in power stations are very large, and some can generate hundreds of thousands of **watts** per second.

(*See also:* **Geothermal power** and **Hydroelecric power**.)

▼ **Generator** – The nature of electric generation is shown in this reproduction of a 19th-century device similar to the one in which the principle was first discovered. A rod of iron is pushed in and out of a coil. The electricity produced is registered on a meter.

Geothermal power

Electric power produced by using the natural steam found near some volcanoes. The steam is used under pressure to turn the shaft of a **generator**.

Ground

A safe place to conduct electrical **current**. Grounding, or earthing, is a way of conducting any unwanted positive electrical **charge** safely into the ground. A **lightning conductor** is a grounding **wire**.

A grounding wire is connected to the metal parts of some **appliances**, such as **stoves** and heaters, to provide a safe escape route for electricity in the event of a **live wire** accidentally touching the metal.

The live wire of a **power supply** can give a bad **electric shock** if touched. If a piece of equipment has a metal case, then there is a small risk that the live wire may touch the case, making the case live also. To prevent this, the case is grounded. Equipment with a plastic (insulating) case does not normally need a ground wire. (*See also:* **Neutral wire**.)

Halogen lamp

A lamp made of a **wire filament** inside a very small bulb filled with a 'halogen' gas such as iodine or bromine. The halogen gas allows the filament to burn hotter and therefore give out a whiter light than ordinary lights. Halogen lamps also use less **energy**, last much longer and do not grow dim with use compared with ordinary (**incandescent**) **light bulbs**.

▼ **Halogen lamp** – A halogen bulb is a type of filament bulb.

Glass bulb containing gas

Filament

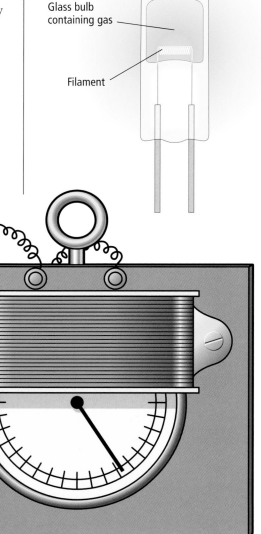

Heating, electric

When a large **current** passes through a thin **wire**, the wire gets hot. It is a heating **element**. A heating element changes **electrical energy** into heat **energy**. The material chosen as the heating element is designed to slow down the flow of electricity and therefore cause as much heat to be produced as possible. The metal must also be able to glow red hot but not melt. Nichrome (a mixture of the metals nickel and chromium) is a common metal used for this task.

Heating elements provide good control over the heat given out, they are cheap and they give out clean heat.

The amount of heat produced by a wire is related to the current flowing in the wire. The larger the current, the more the heat given out.

When the heater is switched on, the current flows through the heating element. The amount of electricity can be controlled by a simple **switch**, called a thermostat.

When a wire carries a large current compared with its size, it can give out both heat and light. A heater needs to give out as much heat as possible, but light is not wanted. The orange glow you see is unwanted light. Heating elements are therefore designed to glow as little as possible.

Appliances that use heating elements

Heating elements can be of many kinds, depending on where they are needed, but the **circuit** is always the same.

Here are some common places where heating elements are found: **toasters**, electric kettles, electric blankets, electric heaters, electric water heaters, electric showers, electric **irons**, hot plates and ovens, and electric storage heaters for central heating.

▲ **Heating, electric** – The principle of a radiant heater.

Hot air rises from the heating element and circulates in the room.

Cooler air is taken in.

▲▶ **Heating, electric** – The principle of a convector heater.

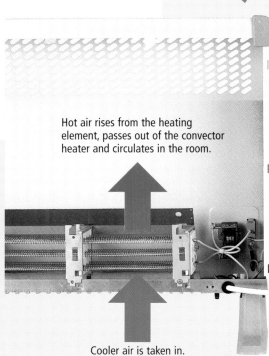

Hot air rises from the heating element, passes out of the convector heater and circulates in the room.

Cooler air is taken in.

Hot (wire)
(*See:* **Live wire**.)

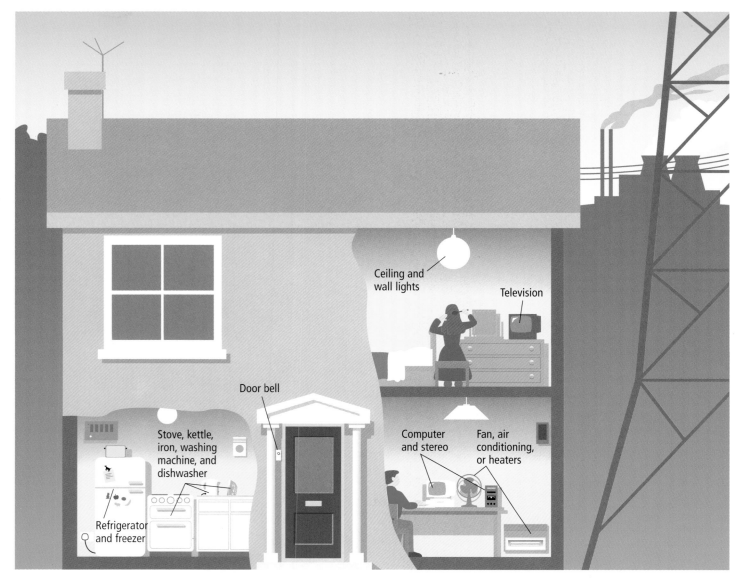

Ceiling and wall lights

Television

Door bell

Stove, kettle, iron, washing machine, and dishwasher

Refrigerator and freezer

Computer and stereo

Fan, air conditioning, or heaters

Household electricity, power supply

The **electricity** supply that is delivered to homes, schools and offices. It is 240 **volts** (V) AC (**alternating current**) to most households in Europe and Australasia. In North America most households only have a 120V AC supply, although those who run larger **appliances** needing more **power** can also have a 240V supply.

The electricity provided by the utility company can be used directly for lights, heaters and many other electrical purposes. Other devices, especially electronic ones, need to have a lower voltage and some need a DC (**direct current**) supply. The

power supply is converted either inside the **plug** or in the device itself using a **transformer** and a **rectifier**.

The key to understanding how and why power is supplied at 120V or 240V is to realise that we demand a large amount of power to our homes. With coffee-makers, heaters, showers and all the other kinds of domestic appliances going at the same time, a household can demand 50 **kilowatts** (kW) or even more. This is a very substantial amount of power.

Power is supplied by a combination of **current** and **voltage**. To get power into a home, you could use fat **cables** and have

▲ **Household electricity** – Every room in the house uses electricity. Bedrooms use electricity for lighting and small appliances such as radios and TVs. Main rooms use electricity much more intensively, for cooking and ventilation, for lighting, for major appliances such as washing machines, dryers, refrigerators, freezers, and for TV and radio. Some homes also heat by electricity.

a low voltage. But fat cables are expensive and difficult to use. The power cable coming into your home would need to be the size of a hosepipe. Imagine trying to bend a metal cable of this size. It would be impossible. There is also a much greater waste of power from a low-voltage supply.

But if you increase the voltage, the current and therefore the cable

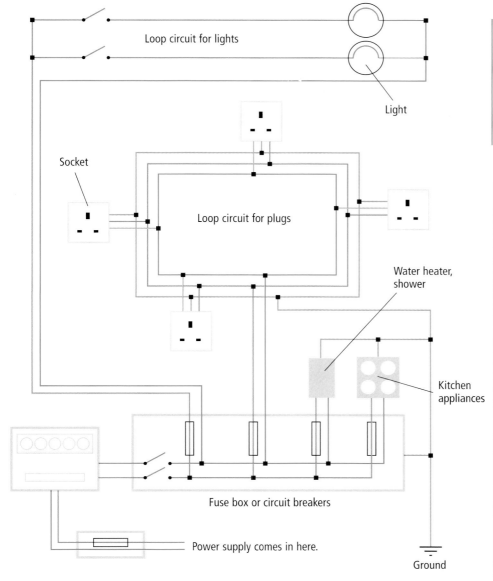

Loop circuit for lights

Light

Socket

Loop circuit for plugs

Water heater, shower

Kitchen appliances

Fuse box or circuit breakers

Power supply comes in here.

Ground

▲ **Household electricity** – A house or apartment is typically provided with two kinds of electricity supply. Both are parallel circuits. One circuit, with thinner cables, is used for lighting; the other, using thicker cables, is for the wall sockets. They are both connected to the supply from the utility company by a switch and a fuse box or through contact breakers.

thickness can be reduced. High-voltage cables also waste far less power. That is the reason why higher voltages are used rather than higher currents.

While higher voltages are efficient, they do pose more of a safety hazard. Touching a live cable can result in **electric shock**. However, this danger is reduced by putting simple safety measures in place. For example, safety plugs with good insulation are used to connect **appliances** to wall **sockets**. (*See also:* **Circuit breaker**.)

The household supply is connected to light fixtures and wall sockets as a **parallel circuit**. That allows many appliances to be used at the same time.

Hydroelectric power

Power produced by using water to turn the shaft of a **generator**. The amount of **energy** in flowing water is a combination of the amount of water and the speed at which it is travelling. This means that a small river flowing over a steep waterfall and a large river flowing over a

gently sloping plain can both be used for generating power. Because a constant supply of **electricity** is needed throughout the year, and the flow in rivers varies with the seasons, many hydroelectric power stations are provided with reservoirs.

I

Immersion heater

An **appliance** containing an electric **heating element** that heats up water.

An immersion heater contains a long heating element that goes right to the bottom of a large cylindrical tank of water. The **wire** of the element is in a pipe-like casing that keeps the heating wire away from the water. Between the wire and the case is air. Air is an **insulator**. When electricity flows, the wire heats the air, which in turn heats the case of the element. The hot casing heats the water.

Immersion heaters can be used in homes to provide hot water.

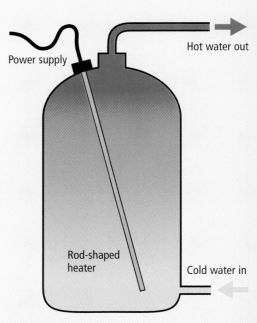

Power supply

Hot water out

Rod-shaped heater

Cold water in

▲ **Immersion heater** – This diagram shows how an immersion heater works.

Incandescent

If something gets very hot, it gives out a bright light as well as heat. When it does this, it is said to be incandescent.

A **filament** in an ordinary (incandescent) **light bulb** is cold when there is no **current** passing through it. When the current flows, the metal filament gets very hot and releases a bright white light. That is why it is called an incandescent light bulb.

Induction

The way in which **electricity** can be caused to flow in a **wire** by moving an iron rod through a coil. (*See also:* **Electromagnet**.)

Insulator

A material that does not allow **current electricity** to flow through it. That is, it does not conduct electricity. Usually, insulators are also poor **conductors** of heat. However, insulators can carry a **charge** of **static electricity** on their surfaces.

The difference in conductivity between an insulator and a conductor is very large. This property is used in the design of all electrical equipment. Since an insulator cannot conduct current electricity, insulated **wire** cannot **short circuit**. A **flex** therefore contains strands of copper wire (the conductors of electricity) separated by plastic sheathing (the insulators).

Many insulating materials are also used in **circuits**. Plastic is the most commonly used, but paper and ceramics are also used in some **components**, such as **capacitors**. Most fabrics are good insulators, and some electric **irons** still use woven cotton coverings for wires because there is a danger that the hot iron could accidentally be placed on a plastic wire and melt it, producing a short circuit.

Most gases are insulators. This is a particularly important and useful property. Dry air, for example, is a good insulator, allowing bare electricity **cables** to hang between **pylons** and **utility poles** without risk of the electricity shorting to the ground.

It is possible to make an insulator break down and conduct electricity, but only under extreme conditions. That happens when a large **spark**, such as **lightning**, occurs.

Although many liquids are conductors, most pure liquids are insulators. For example, pure water is an insulator, but tap water, which contains minerals dissolved in it, conducts electricity. Liquids can also flow around insulators, making a thin conducting film on the surface. That is why it is dangerous to touch a wet **plug** even though the plug is made of insulating plastic. (*See also:* **Socket**.)

Integrated circuit

Also called IC, microchip, **silicon chip**, or just chip, an integrated circuit is a sliver, or chip, of silicon on which are etched all the **components** needed to make a working **circuit**. No internal connecting **wires** are used.

Integrated circuits are used in all electronic devices, not only because they are extremely small and reliable, but also because they are relatively cheap. (*See also:* **Semi-conductor**.)

Iron

A small **appliance** that is used to remove the creases from clothes. It uses an electric **element** the heat output of which is controlled by a device called a thermostat.

The thermostat may have several heat settings. The higher the heat setting, the more electricity is flowing. If too high a heat setting is used, some fabrics will melt or burn.

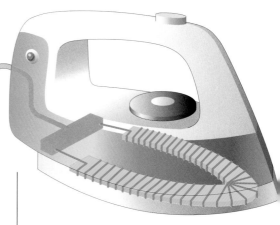

▲ **Iron** – The heating element is highlighted in red on this diagram.

J

Junction of wires

A place where **wires** are joined together to allow **electricity** to move between them.

K

Kilowatt (kW)

A useful measure of **power**. It equals 1,000 **watts**.

L

Leyden jar

A glass jar with a sheet of metal foil on the inside of the glass and another sheet wrapped around the outside. A nail leads from the inner foil through the cork stopper. When a **charged** object is touched to the nail, the charge is held on the inner foil and remains there until the nail and the outer foil are touched. Then it discharges, producing an electric **current**.

To demonstrate the effect, soon after the Leyden jar was invented, 700 monks were persuaded to join hands in a big circle. One monk then touched the nail of the Leyden jar, and the monk at the other end of the line touched the outside foil. The shock caused all 700 monks to leap into the air.

The Leyden jar was later developed into the **capacitor**, an important electronic **component** for storing **electricity**. (*See also:* **Electricity and its history**.)

Light bulb

A gas-filled glass bulb containing a thin **wire** that gets very hot and shines brightly when **electricity** flows through it.

The fine wire is called a **filament**. The wire used for the filament is a special metal (usually tungsten) that will glow brightly – or incandesce – without melting (*see:* **Incandescent**). The filament gives out light that is yellower than natural light.

The filament is made of a tightly coiled wire. The longer the coil, the more light is given out. Thus, a 25 **watt** (W) light bulb has a shorter filament than a 100W bulb.

If the filament were left exposed to the air, it would quickly burn out. Filaments, therefore, have to be protected from the air, which is why they are enclosed in a glass bulb. The original bulbs had the air sucked out before they were sealed. The bulb shape was needed to withstand the pressure of air.

Modern bulbs have a non-flammable (inert) gas like argon in them to balance out the pressure from the outside air and allow the glass to be thin.

The filament has a life of perhaps 1,000 hours. Two things shorten

▼▶ **Light bulb** – Light bulbs are all made with a glass bulb filled with argon or a similar gas under low pressure. Nearly all low-voltage flashlight bulbs have a screw fitting. Many household bulbs also have a screw fitting, but some have a bayonet fitting. A few – such as halogen bulbs – have two prongs as contacts. In the case of the screw fitting, one contact is on the base, and the other is the screw; in the case of the bayonet fitting, there are two contacts on the base. Each kind of bulb will only fit in its appropriate holder.

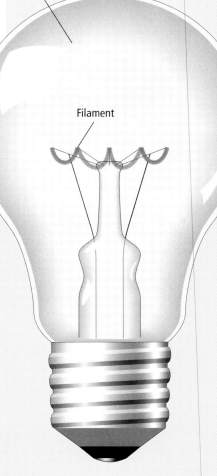

Argon gas

Glass bulb

Filament

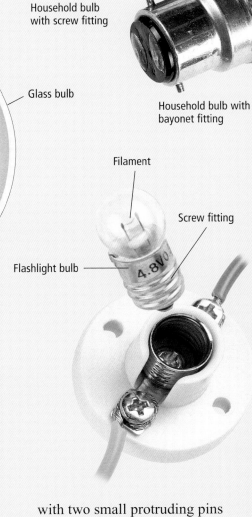

Household bulb with screw fitting

Household bulb with bayonet fitting

Filament

Screw fitting

Flashlight bulb

4.8V

the life of the filament. The first is frequent switching on and off, since the expansion and contraction involved each time wears out the wire metal. The filament also becomes thinner and more fragile as it gets older, so the slightest tap can cause it to break.

Light bulbs have two types of fittings. Small **flashlight**-type light bulbs and room light bulbs have an Edison Screw (ES) fitting. Other light bulbs have a fitting with two small protruding pins (*see:* **Contacts**). It is called a bayonet fitting.

Incandescent light bulbs are not very efficient. Considerable amounts of **electrical energy** are lost as heat in a light bulb. That is the reason why an incandescent light bulb is hot to the touch. For longer life and more economic operation, **fluorescent** 'energy'-saving' lights are often used. (*See also:* **Arc light**; **Halogen lamp; Photoelectric cell**.)

Light-emitting diode (LED)

A **semi-conductor** (a kind of **transistor**) that gives out light when an electric **current** flows through it. Light-emitting **diodes** (LEDs) do not give out much light, but the light is usually of a single colour (not a combination of colours, as in white light).

LEDs consume little **power** for the light they give out because they do not heat up. That means they can be driven by batteries if necessary. They are used as indicators and can show if an **appliance** is on or off, or they can display the volume level in a **radio**. They are also used in some car rear brake lights.

▼ **LED** – LEDs are sometimes used for rear lighting on bicycles.

In this part of the cloud, water droplets carry a positive charge.

The lower part of the cloud has a negative charge.

The ground below the cloud is positively charged.

▲ **Lightning** – Lightning strikes when sufficient difference in charge builds up between a cloud and the ground, or between two layers of a cloud.

Lightning

A natural **spark** produced between charged layers of cloud or between a cloud and the ground.

Lightning occurs because different kinds of electrical **charge** build up inside a thundercloud. The same kind of process happens in the air as when two insulating materials are rubbed together. Opposite charges build up on the surfaces of each material until there is enough charge to make a spark.

The rubbing action in a cloud is produced by the raindrops that swirl around inside a thundercloud.

A large positive charge builds in the upper part of the cloud and a large negative charge in the lower cloud.

A cloud-to-ground lightning flash contains at least two strokes. A leader stroke sets out from the cloud to the ground and it causes a return stroke to rise from the ground to the cloud. When these strokes meet, the cloud is **short circuited** to the ground, and a bright stroke of high current passes between cloud and ground.

The difference in **voltage** between cloud and ground may be several hundred million **volts**, and **currents** may be as much as 20,000 **amps**. The flash heats the air within a few milliseconds, making it expand. This expansion makes the sound we call thunder.

Live wire

The **wire** connected to the positive side of an **electricity** supply. The live wire in a UK **household wire** or **cable** is always coloured brown or red. Other countries use different colour schemes. (*See also:* **Ground**; **Neutral wire**; **Plug**; **Socket**.)

Load

A word used to describe a **component** or **appliance** that runs from a **power supply**.

M

Magnet (permanent, bar, horseshoe)

A solid that attracts iron. A magnet has two ends where the strength of **magnetism** is greatest. They are called the **north pole** and the **south pole**. Similar **poles** push each other apart (they repel); unlike poles attract (*see:* **Attractive force** and **Repulsive force**).

It does not matter what size the magnet is; it will always have a north and a south pole. So if you cut a magnet in half, both pieces will still each have a north and a south pole.

The Earth behaves like a giant bar magnet. If you tie a thread around the middle of a bar magnet and then hold the magnet by the thread, the magnet will swing around until the south pole of the magnet is pointing to the Earth's magnetic north. That is the principle of the **compass**.

The poles of magnets are labelled according to how they behave in the Earth's magnetic field. Thus the south pole of a magnet seeks the Earth's north pole, and a north pole of a magnet seeks the Earth's south pole. Magnetic lines of **force** leave the north-seeking pole and flow to the south-seeking pole of a magnet.

Magnets can also be permanent, created from metal in the Earth's magnetic field. Ironstones can be permanent magnets. Lodestone is a naturally magnetic form of iron that was used to make the first compasses. Stroking a piece of iron or mild steel with a magnetic object causes the iron or steel to become magnetised. This magnetism will not weaken, so it is called permanent magnetism.

Temporary magnets can also be made by passing an electric **current** through a coil of **wire**. That is the principle of the **electromagnet**, the most widely used form of magnet in the world. Electromagnets are used to pick up scrap steel, to run **solenoids**, in loudspeakers, to generate **electricity**, and in a wide range of **appliances**, such as **motors** and computers.

The force that is created around a magnet is known as a **magnetic field**. This 'field' is invisible, but can always be detected by a compass. The shape of the magnetic field is shown by means of curving lines going from the north to south poles.

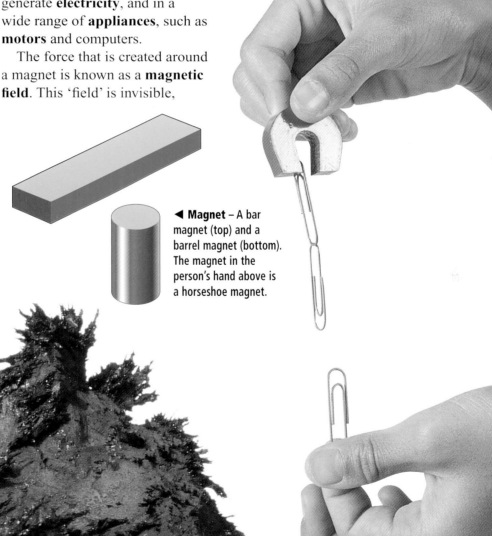

▼ **Magnet** – A magnet will attract magnetic materials such as iron and mild steel. The magnetism will be transferred from one object to another, so that a whole line of objects can be held by a single magnet.

◄ **Magnet** – A bar magnet (top) and a barrel magnet (bottom). The magnet in the person's hand above is a horseshoe magnet.

◄ **Magnet** – Lodestone, or magnetite, is a naturally magnetic rock. This rock sample has been coated in iron filings to show its magnetic effect.

Magnetic field

The region over which a **magnet** has a noticeable effect. The field is easily demonstrated in a bar magnet by sprinkling iron filings onto a sheet of paper over the magnet and then tapping the paper. It can also be shown using a **compass**.

Magnetic pole

The place where the **magnetic field** enters or leaves a **magnet**. Because the lines of **force** concentrate at the **poles**, they are the most powerful parts of the magnet.

Magnetic poles can be either **north poles** or **south poles**. The field leaves the north pole and enters the south pole. The Earth's magnetic poles are not in quite the same positions as its geographic poles.

Magnetism

The **force** that attracts and repels iron and some other materials. (*See also:* **Attractive force** and **Repulsive force**.)

Magnetism is produced by permanent **magnets** or **electromagnets**. Permanent magnets and electromagnets influence the space around them. That is where the **magnetic field** is found. (*See also:* **Ørsted** and **Ørsted, Hans Christian**.)

Meter

An instrument that indicates what is happening inside a **circuit**.

A meter consists of a coil of **wire** equipped with a pointer and suspended between a pair of small permanent **magnets**. When an electric **current** flows in the coil, it becomes an **electromagnet**. It interacts with the **magnetism** of the permanent magnets and causes the coil and pointer to twist. The amount of twisting movement

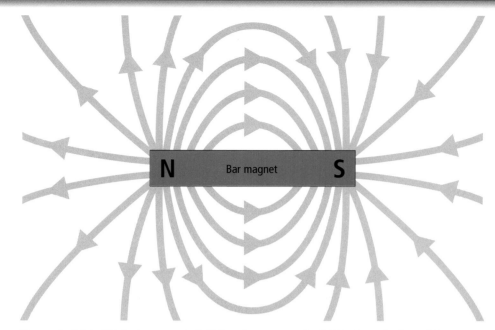

▲ **Magnetic field** – This is the magnetic field for a bar magnet. The field is shown by lines of force that leave the north-seeking pole and go to the south-seeking pole.

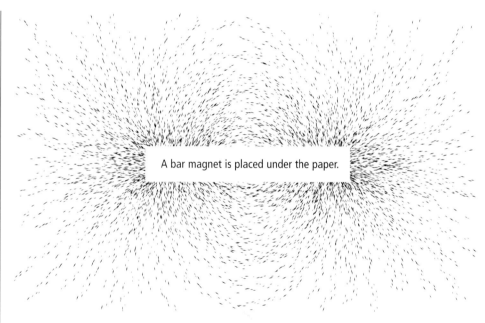

A bar magnet is placed under the paper.

▲ **Magnetic field** – This demonstrates the way in which lines of force can be found by scattering iron filings on a paper and then placing a bar magnet under the paper. Compare it to the diagram above.

varies with the electricity flowing in the coil.

Meters can be built to indicate current, **voltage**, or **resistance**. A meter is as essential to an electrician as a stethoscope is to a doctor. It can be used to find out what is happening in a circuit. For example, a meter can show if a circuit is broken. It can be used to test a **battery** or the **household** **power supply**. Meters can also be used to investigate the current in an electronic circuit.

An electrician's general purpose meter is often called a **circuit tester**, or a multimeter, because by simply turning a dial on the front, a wide range (multi) of measurements of a circuit can be made. (*See also:* **Ammeter** and **Ohmmeter**.)

Motor, electric

A device that converts **electricity** into a turning movement. Most motors have a spindle that is used to drive a machine. Motors can work on DC (**direct current**) or AC (**alternating current**) supplies. Motors can be 'used backwards' to generate electricity.

The electric motor is one of the most efficient devices – far more efficient than a **light bulb**, for example. You can tell this because a working motor rarely gets hot. This shows that little **energy** is wasted as heat.

The motor is an example of a device making use of both electricity and **magnetism**.

The first very simple motor was built by British scientist Michael **Faraday** in the middle of the 19th century. It was the foundation of all motors and **generators** now in use.

A DC motor, such as a small motor that runs from **battery power**, contains a coil of **wire** on a spindle. The spindle, which sits in bearings and can spin freely, can then be connected to a machine such as a CD player.

The coil is surrounded by a powerful permanent **magnet**. When the electricity supply is switched on, the wires in the coil create a **magnetic field** and interact with the field of the permanent magnet. That makes the spindle turn. By using a special collar on the shaft, the motor can be made to continue turning.

The amount of power developed in the coil depends on the strength of the permanent magnet and the number of turns of wire in the coil.

In most larger motors the outer magnet is also an **electromagnet**. It can be made much stronger than a permanent magnet. As a result, a motor appears to contain one set of coils inside another. The electricity supply powers both sets of coils.

The earliest motors ran on direct current (DC) and those in cars and in portable equipment still do. However, most modern motors run on AC because the design can be simpler and the motor can be made more reliable.

▲ **Motor** – Electric trains and trams are powered by electric motors.

▼ **Motor** – A simple motor and how it works.

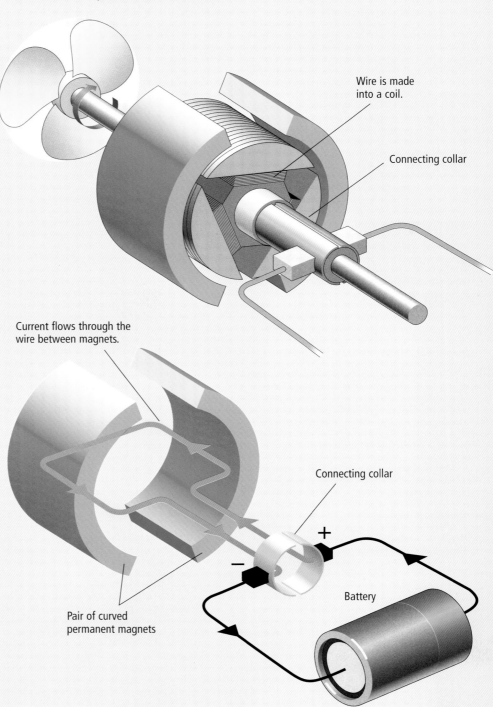

Wire is made into a coil.

Connecting collar

Current flows through the wire between magnets.

Connecting collar

Pair of curved permanent magnets

Battery

Multimeter
(*See:* **Circuit tester**.)

N

Negative terminal
The negative end of a **battery**. In a tubular **dry cell** or battery the negative terminal is the flat end. In a car battery the negative terminal is marked by a minus (–) sign. The negative terminal usually has a thick **cable** connecting it to the body of the car. (*See also:* **Positive terminal**.)

Neon lighting
Neon is a colourless gas that gives out a red light when a **current** of electricity flows through it.

Neon is found naturally in very small amounts in the air. It is mixed up with other gases such as oxygen and nitrogen. Neon can be collected from the air by cooling the air down until the neon gas becomes a liquid.

Neon is used mainly for decorative lighting such as shop signs. The glass tubes can be bent into a variety of shapes.

In some displays neon is used to create red light, and other gases make other colours of light. You can see this in the picture on the right.

Mercury vapour in a neon lamp produces a blue light; helium in amber glass glows gold; blue light in yellow glass glows green; and combinations of gases give out white light.

Neutral wire
The **wire** connected to the negative side of the electricity supply. The neutral wire is coloured blue or black. (*See also:* **Ground**; **Live wire**; **Plug**; **Socket**.)

▶ **Neon lighting** – Neon lighting in Las Vegas.

North pole
The north-seeking end of a **magnet** when suspended in the Earth's **magnetic field**. It is the end of the magnet from which the lines of **force** leave. (*See also:* **Pole**; **Magnetic pole**; **South pole**.)

O

Ohm
The unit of **resistance**. It is named after Georg Simon **Ohm**. (*See also:* **Ohm's Law**.)

Ohm, Georg Simon
A German mathematics professor (1789–1854) who, in the early 19th century, studied the way electric **current** flows through a **circuit**. In 1827 he found a relationship between the **voltage** applied, the **resistance** of the **components**, and the current flowing in the circuit. It is now called **Ohm's Law**. (*See also:* **Electricity and its history**.)

Ohmmeter
A **meter** designed to measure **resistance**. It is usually part of a multimeter or **circuit tester**. (*See also:* **Ammeter**.)

Ohm's Law
A law developed by Georg Simon **Ohm** in 1827 that relates the **voltage**, **current** and **resistance** of

a **circuit**. It is one of the most important laws in **electricity** and electronics.

This is Ohm's Law:

If a **resistor** has a value of R **ohms** and carries a current of I **amp**, then the voltage V across the resistor is equal to the product of I and R, or

$$V = IR$$

Ørsted (O)

The unit for measuring **magnetism**. (*See also:* **Ørsted, Hans Christian**.)

Ørsted, Hans Christian

A professor of physics in Copenhagen, Denmark (1777–1851), who, in 1820, demonstrated that an electric **current** flowing in a **wire** would cause a **compass** needle to move. In this way he showed that **electricity** and **magnetism** are connected. Ørsted has given his name to the unit of measuring magnetism, the **Ørsted**. (*See also:* **Electricity and its history**.)

Overload

A situation in which the demand for **electricity** exceeds the supply. Overloads can happen in the home and on a larger scale.

An overload in the home occurs if too many devices are being used at the same time, or if one device has a **short circuit**, causing an unexpectedly high **current** to flow. **Fuses** and **circuit breakers** are designed to disconnect the **power supply** should this happen.

The same can happen in, say, a city. In this case giant circuit breakers in the generating supply can cause complete districts within a city to lose **power**. This is called a **blackout**. In some situations the power company can see a problem coming and can lower the voltage. This makes lights dim and **appliances** work poorly. It is called a **brownout**.

P

Parallel circuit

An electric **circuit** in which the **components** are connected in parallel (side by side, not in a line), so each component has a direct connection to the **electricity** supply.

In a parallel circuit many components can be fed with the same **voltage**. When one component fails, the rest keep on working.

Many circuits work in this way. The electrical system in a car is a parallel circuit. The 12V **battery** supplies electricity independently to the lights, the engine and the **radio**, so that you can listen to the radio with the engine turned off or run the engine with the radio turned off.

The **household power supply** is another example of a parallel circuit. All of the wall **sockets** are connected to two loops of **wire** that go around the house. The ceiling lights are connected to two more loops of thinner wires.

In a parallel circuit you can keep adding electrical devices without affecting those already operating. But the more you add, the more **power** you need to supply them. That is, the electric **current** supplied must be equal to the total current used by each of the devices in the circuit (known as the **load**).

If there are many devices connected to a parallel circuit (for example, electric heater, oven, washing machine, water heater), a very large amount of power may be used. As a result, the thickness of the **cables** must match the total load that is expected. To make sure there is never an **overload**, causing the cables to heat up and risking a fire, the supply to most parallel circuits has **fuses** or **circuit breakers** placed in it.

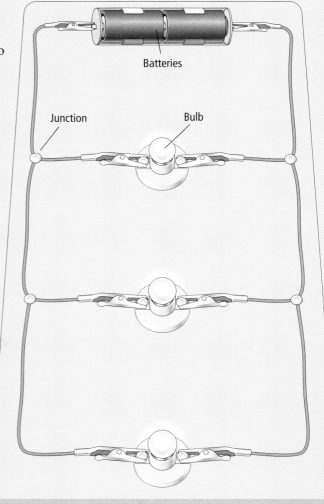

▶ **Parallel circuit** – Every load (in this case the bulbs) is connected directly to the power supply (in this case the batteries).

Photoelectric cell

A **cell** that reacts to light by producing **electricity**.

When light falls on some materials, they change from being **insulators** to being **conductors**. As a result, they can be used as **switches**. A **circuit** is made with the photoelectric cell placed between the **power supply** and the **load** – for example, between the **household electricity** supply and a porch light. As dusk approaches, the light falling on the photoelectric cell changes, and the conductivity of the cell increases. This 'automatically' switches on the porch light. At sunrise the conductivity reverses again and the light goes out.

The photoelectric effect was discovered in 1887 by a German scientist, Heinrich Rudolf Hertz.

Photovoltaic cell, solar cell

An **electricity**-producing **cell**. It relies on the fact that, when light falls on some materials, they will convert the light to electricity. The solar cell is an example of this kind of cell. The cell is made of a **semi-conductor** sheet stuck to a metal plate. When light falls on the semi-conductor, the cell acts as a source of electricity.

The **electric power** generated by this kind of cell is low for its size. As a result, solar cells are usually built in the form of panels, where the electric power produced varies with the size of the panel and the intensity of the sunlight falling on it. Cells of this kind do not work well on cloudy days. (*See also:* **Solar power**.)

Piezoelectricity

Electricity produced by pressure on a device.

When some crystals are squeezed, they develop a positive **charge** on one side of the crystal and a negative charge on the opposite side.

This also works in reverse. When a **voltage** is placed across the crystal, it changes shape.

Applying a rapidly changing voltage to a crystal such as a wafer of silicon can make it vibrate. A rapidly vibrating pressure can cause the crystal to produce a rapidly changing electric voltage.

The piezoelectric effect is used in electronic devices such as 'quartz' clocks and watches.

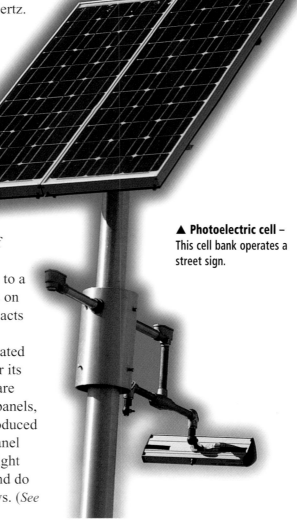

▲ **Photoelectric cell –** This cell bank operates a street sign.

Plug, electrical

A device that allows you to connect and disconnect electrical devices safely and easily to a **power supply**.

Plugs are made of insulating materials (*see:* **Insulator**). Some plugs have a **fuse** built into them. It allows safe control of any local **overload**.

In many cases people want to move their electrical equipment from place to place. For example, they may need to move the vacuum cleaner from one room to another. To do this conveniently, there must be a safe way of connecting and disconnecting an **appliance** from its source of **power**. That is the purpose of the plug and wall **socket**.

Plugs are found on all electrical appliances. They are the easiest way of connecting and disconnecting appliances to the **power supply**.

It is important to understand how a plug and socket work because this understanding leads to greater safety in their use.

Both plug and socket are made of shock-resistant insulating plastic. They are also made of a plastic that will not burn when it gets hot. That is important in case there is an electrical fault. Plugs are also designed to be a convenient shape for handling. A plug must always fit firmly into the socket. To make this possible, the socket contains springy metal clips to hold the plug pins firmly in place (*see:* **Contacts**).

The plug has two **wires** (**live** and **neutral**) that carry the electric **current** and often a third safety wire called the ground wire. To make use of it, some plugs have a third pin. The ground carries no electric current; the other two pins carry the electric current.

To make sure that the electricity

◀▲▼ **Plug** – Many countries have their own types of plug. From the United States (below), Australia (above), and the United Kingdom (left).

supply is connected correctly, a plug must always be wired correctly.

It can be dangerous to wire plugs. It should only be done by someone with experience in what they are doing.

Pole
The attracting or repelling end of a **magnet** (*see:* **Attractive force** and **Repulsive force**). Magnets have **north poles** and **south poles**. (*See also:* **Magnetic pole**.)

Positive terminal
The positive end of a **battery**. In a tubular **dry cell** the positive terminal has a small bump. In a car battery the positive terminal is marked by a plus (+) sign. The positive terminal is also usually covered. (*See also:* **Negative terminal**.)

Potentiometer
Another word for **variable resistor**.

Power

A way of talking about the amount of **electrical energy** used.

All electrical equipment uses power. The amount of power used is measured in **watts** (W). Devices that use a large amount of power are always run off the **household power supply**, not from **batteries**.

A small electric light uses about 25W; a large electric light uses 100W; a small **flashlight** bulb may use 1.5W.

Appliances such as stoves and heaters use much more power. For example, the heating ring of an electric stove may use 1,000W (1kW – one **kilowatt**). An electric heater may consume 2,000W (2kW) or more. A water heater has to heat water very fast and may consume as much as 9kW.

The more power taken by an electric **circuit**, the thicker the supply **cables** have to be. That is why the cable used to connect an electric heater to the power supply is thicker than the cable used to connect a table lamp.

In a battery-run circuit the more power that is used, the faster a battery runs down.

Power is equal to **amps** multiplied by **volts**. For example, if a **motor** is connected to a 9V battery and uses 0.5W of power, we can easily work out how much **current** (amps) is flowing in the **wires**:

$$\text{Power (W)} =$$
$$\text{Voltage (V)} \times \text{Current (A)}$$
$$0.5 = 9 \times A$$
$$A = 0.5/9 \ (0.055)$$

The motor uses 0.055A of current.

Calculations like these allow electricians to work out the correct size of cable needed to connect appliances, the size of the **fuse** that should be used, and what kind of battery is needed if the equipment is to be portable.

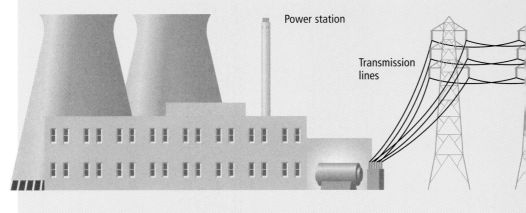

Power station

Transmission lines

▲ **Power supply** – Power supplies consist of generating stations whose power is distributed by a grid of transmission lines.

Power-generating station, power station

A building in which **electricity** is made or generated.

They are some of the most important buildings in the modern world because so much of what we do depends on a reliable supply of electricity. Even when we use other forms of **energy**, such as gas central heating, the control equipment for the heating requires electricity.

About four-tenths of all the energy used in an industrial country is used in the form of electricity.

The first power stations were built in the last part of the 19th century. At first they were only able to supply enough **power** for a few hundred **light bulbs**. These early power stations were steam powered. Most power stations are still run on steam today.

Inside a power station there are one or more **generators**. They turn chemical energy in the fuel into heat energy, which turns water into steam and then into energy of movement. By turning the shaft of the generator, movement is converted into electricity for homes, schools, offices and factories.

Generator shafts are usually connected to angled blades called turbine blades. They act somewhat like a propeller. When high pressure steam hits the blades, they move and turn the shaft.

Steam is normally provided by heating water using coal, oil, or natural gas (**fossil fuels**) as a fuel. Nuclear energy is also sometimes used as a heat source. There are also some environmentally friendly ways to turn the generator shaft, such as using **wind power** and water power (**hydroelectric power**); but they only provide small amounts of power compared with the traditional fossil fuels.

A large power station can produce over 1 billion **kilowatts** of electrical power.

Power from the power station is supplied to customers through **transmission lines**. The **cables** carry AC (**alternating current**) electricity at very high voltages. It has to be stepped down with **transformers** in **substations** before it can be used. A network of transmission lines connecting power stations to consumers is called an **electricity grid** (also called utility grid or power grid).

(*See also:* **Geothermal power**; **Solar power**; **Static, static electricity**.)

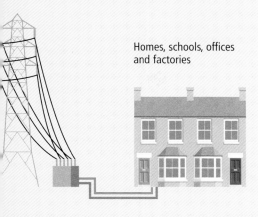

Homes, schools, offices and factories

Power supply

The **power** that enters homes, schools, factories and so on. For historical reasons the power supply is usually 120V in North America and 240V elsewhere. In North America it is common for most household equipment to run from 120V, but there is also a separate 240V supply for large **appliances** like washing machines.

(*See also:* **Electricity grid**; **Generator**; **Household electricity**; **Transmission lines**.)

Primary battery, cell

A device for changing chemical energy into **electrical energy**. It can only be used once. It cannot be recharged. Once the chemicals are used up, the **battery** or **cell** must be safely disposed of. They cannot be reused.

Economy zinc–carbon and long-life **alkaline batteries** or cells are primary devices. (*See also:* **Rechargeable battery, cell** and **Secondary battery, cell**.)

Pylons

Metal frames used to support **transmission lines** as they cross open countryside. Local distribution of **electricity** in towns and cities uses **utility poles** or underground **cables**. (*See also:* **Electricity grid**.)

Electricity cable

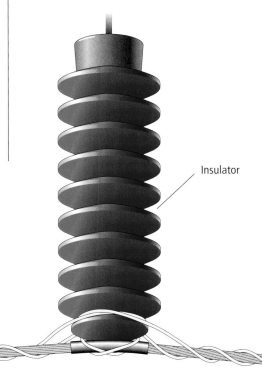

▼ **Pylons** – The pylons are metal frames, which are naturally grounded. To keep the transmission lines insulated from the pylons, special ceramic insulators are used.

Insulator

▼ **Pylons** – Pylons carry high-voltage transmission lines across the countryside.

R

Radio

A device that can detect certain waves of **energy** in the air called radio waves. A simple radio consists of an **antenna** to pick up signals, a **circuit** to make them stronger and an earpiece to change the electrical signals into sound.

When you turn on a radio, it detects the energy in the radio waves and converts them into electrical signals that flow to a loudspeaker.

At a radio station people talk or play music into microphones. The sound is then changed into electrical signals that move to a transmitter. It is a device that changes the **electrical energy** into radio waves that spread out in all directions. (*See also:* **Amplifier**; **Coil**; **Current**; **Transistor**; **Variable resistor**.)

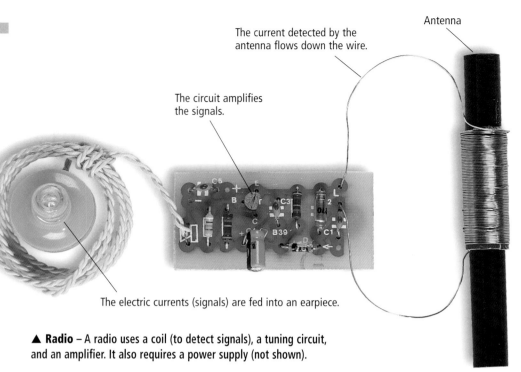

The circuit amplifies the signals.

The current detected by the antenna flows down the wire.

Antenna

The electric currents (signals) are fed into an earpiece.

▲ **Radio** – A radio uses a coil (to detect signals), a tuning circuit, and an amplifier. It also requires a power supply (not shown).

Rechargeable battery, cell

A **battery**, or **cell**, that can be used more than once. Rechargeable batteries and cells have to be **charged** in the first place; they do not contain chemicals that can make **electricity**. Instead, they contain materials that store electricity. Rechargeable batteries and cells are also called **secondary batteries** and cells.

Rectifier

A device for changing an **alternating current (AC)** into a **direct current (DC)**.

Repulsive force

The pushing **force** of two similar **magnetic poles**, or places, with the same electric **charge**. (*Compare with:* **Attractive force**.)

Resistance

The ease with which an electrical **current** flows through a **conductor**. A piece of copper, for example, will allow **electricity** to flow through it more easily than a piece of carbon. The copper has a lower resistance than the carbon. As a result, copper is used for **wires** and carbon is used to make **resistors**. (*See also:* **Ohm**; **Ohmmeter**; **Ohm's Law**.)

Resistor

A small **component** designed to reduce the flow of **electricity** in a **circuit**.

You can recognise a resistor because it usually has a tubular body with brightly coloured rings. The rings are a colour code that shows the value of the resistor.

The effect of a resistor on a circuit is given by **Ohm's Law**.

Resistors are commonly made of finely powdered carbon (graphite) mixed with clay. The resistance depends on the proportion of carbon to clay; the higher the ratio of carbon to clay, the lower the resistance.

Wirewound resistors are made of the metal alloy nichrome (nickel and chromium). It has a higher resistance than most metals. Wirewound resistors can be used to carry larger **currents** than carbon resistors. (*See also:* **Thermistor** and **Variable resistor**.)

Rheostat

A **variable resistor**.

S

Secondary battery, cell

A **rechargeable battery** or **cell**. It has to be **charged** in the first place, but then it can be reused many times. Car **batteries** (**accumulators**) are secondary batteries. Some **dry cells** have the words 'rechargeable' written on them. They are the only cells that can be recharged, and even then only by using a special charger.

Weight for weight, a secondary battery or cell has a lower **power** output than a **primary battery** or cell.

Semi-conductor

A material that will **conduct electricity** in some situations, but not in others. This feature allows precise control of electrical **current**.

A number of different things can influence the flow of electricity. For example, the amount of **voltage** applied or, in the case of a **photovoltaic cell**, how much light falls on the semi-conducting material.

A semi-conductor is made by adding impurities to a material such as silicon or germanium. Silicon is the most widely used, hence the term **silicon chip**.

A semi-conductor is used in electronic **circuits** for the same purposes as a **vacuum tube**, but it is much faster, uses only a small electrical current and is far smaller. In this way a single **integrated circuit**, which incorporates thousands of semi-conductor **components**, can do the work that would once have needed whole buildings full of vacuum tubes and a **power station** to run them. (*See also:* **Light-emitting diode; Thermistor; Transistor**.)

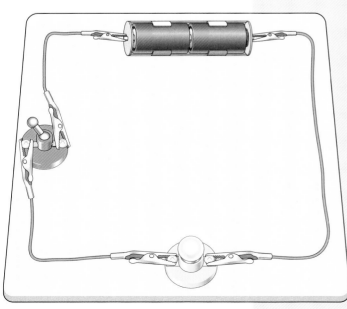

Series circuit

An electrical **circuit** in which all the **components** are connected end to end in a single loop. The **electricity** has only one path it can take.

In a series circuit the electricity can be thought of as flowing from the positive side of the **battery**, through connecting **wires** and loads (for example, a **light bulb** or **buzzer**), through more wires, and back to the negative side of the battery.

When one component fails, the whole circuit stops working. For this reason a series circuit can be used in only a limited number of ways (see the lights on page 40). Most circuits are **parallel circuits**.

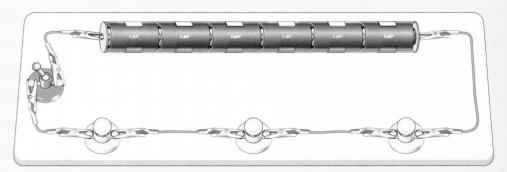

▲ **Series circuit** – A series circuit with six 1.5V batteries and three 3V bulbs. The sum of the voltages match, so the bulbs will shine brightly.

▼ **Series circuit** – The circuit diagram for three bulbs in series.

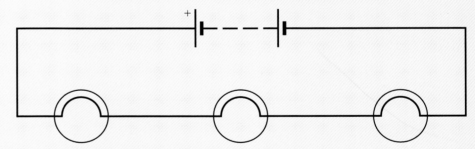

◄ **Series circuit** – This circuit has a bulb connected to a battery through a switch. Notice they are all in a single loop. This must, therefore, be a series circuit.

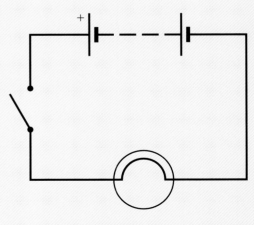

▲ **Series circuit** – This circuit diagram is for one bulb and one switch in series.

▲ **Series circuit** – These lights are all linked together in a chain and so are in series.

Shockley, William B.

Shockley (1910–1989) led the development of the **transistor**. He was born in London, and studied and lived in California. (*See also:* **Electricity and its history**.)

Short circuit

A situation in which, for example, the **positive** and **negative** **terminals** of a **battery** or **power** **supply** are connected directly together, causing a large **current** to flow.

Fuses and **circuit breakers** are designed to break the **circuit** when short circuits occur. (*See also:* **Overload**.)

Silicon chip

A small piece of silicon on which a variety of **semi-conductors** and other **components** are etched. Another term is **integrated circuit**.

Socket

Half of the connecting system that allows you to easily connect and disconnect electric devices. In many cases people want to move their electrical equipment from place to place. For example, they may need to move the vacuum cleaner from one room to another. To do this conveniently, there must be a safe way of connecting and disconnecting an **appliance** from the **power supply**. That is the purpose of the **plug** and socket. Sockets are matched with plugs so that inappropriate devices cannot be connected in error. There are sockets on the back of many appliances and computers. They are very different from wall sockets.

Sockets are made of insulating materials (*see:* **Insulator**). Some sockets have a **switch** built into them. That provides additional safe control of the **electricity**.

Inside a wall socket two **wires** lead off to the **cable** looping around the house that provides the **household power supply** (*see:* **Live wire** and **Neutral wire**). A third wire may be used as a ground.

Solar power

The electrical **power** produced by converting the radiation **energy** of the Sun.

There are two different ways of using the energy from the Sun. A solar **power station** contains many highly polished mirrors that reflect the Sun's rays onto tubes carrying water. The water gets hot enough to produce steam, which is then used to turn the shaft of a **generator**.

Solar panels (**photovoltaic cells**) are made of light-sensitive **semi-conductors** that produce an electric **current** when light falls on them. These panels are used as power sources for satellites, in electronic calculators and in other devices that need only a small amount of power. It is possible to couple many of these cells together

▼ **Solar power** – This is part of a solar generating station (solar farm) in California.

to create larger power outputs, but so far it has proved difficult to make them efficient enough to make electricity economically on a large scale.

Solenoid

A coil of insulated **wire** wound on a tube. When **electricity** flows in the **coil**, a **magnetic field** is created (induced) entirely within the core of the tube. Lines of **force** only occur outside the core at the ends, so the coil behaves like a **magnet**. When the current flows, an iron or mild steel rod is connected inside the core. In effect the core becomes a moving object. A solenoid is used for moving the striker in a chiming door bell or connecting a starter **motor** to a car engine, for example. (*See also:* **Electromagnet**.)

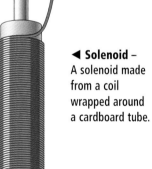

◀ **Solenoid –** A solenoid made from a coil wrapped around a cardboard tube.

South pole

The end of a **magnet** where the lines of **force** arrive. (*See also:* **Magnetic pole**; **North pole**; **Pole**.)

Spark

The sudden flow of **electricity** through the air between two **charged** surfaces. A flash of **lightning** is the world's biggest spark. Small sparks also occur whenever a **switch** is turned and the **contacts** separated or closed. (*See also:* **Static electricity**.)

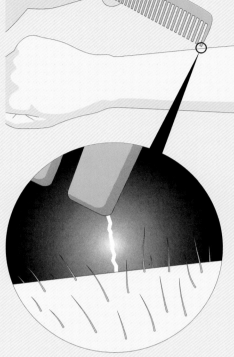

▶ **Spark –** Sparks are readily made by bringing a charged comb close to the skin. You can also feel the attraction because it makes the hairs on your arm stand up straight.

▼ **Spark –** Sparks occur whenever an electrical contact is made or broken. This sparking makes pits in the contacts of switches, for example, and, in time, will wear them out.

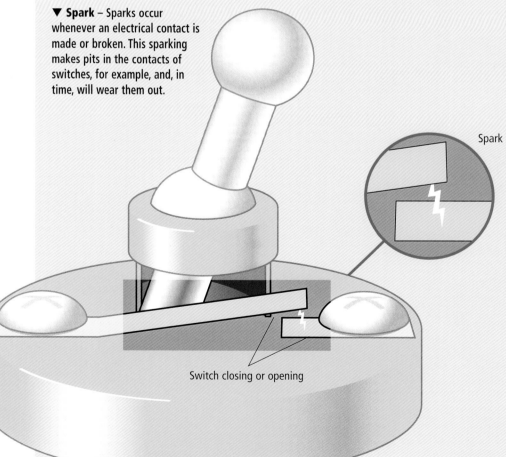

Spark

Switch closing or opening

Static, static electricity

Electricity that builds up on the surfaces of insulating materials (**insulators**) as a result of their being rubbed together. It consists of positive and negatively **charged** surfaces.

Static electricity causes some objects to be attracted to one another (*see:* **Attractive force**). The discharge of static electricity causes a **spark**.

The word static means at rest, and static electricity is electricity at rest. It is like a reservoir of electricity in one place, while an electric **current** is a flow of electricity. Usually this reservoir of electricity occurs on the surface of an insulator.

Static electricity is most often produced unintentionally and is thought to be a nuisance. For example, a build-up of static on a car during dry weather can cause a shock if you touch the door handle. Small pieces of charged material can stick to the surface of objects in the same way as dust sticks to **television** screens. The static charge that builds up when shoes are scuffed on a carpet can reach 20,000 **volts**. The shock that can be produced is not harmful because the current is so low.

Sometimes, enough static electricity builds up for the electric charge to break through the air and produce a large spark. That is what happens when **lightning** strikes. It can be especially hazardous to tall buildings, isolated trees and people standing out in the open. Buildings have to be protected from damage by a lightning rod.

Static can also be produced by sparks created in electric **motors** and car engines. Special **components** – called suppressors – are attached to get rid of this problem.

Static electricity does have some important uses. Some electronic components, such as **capacitors**, store electricity as static. A television tube uses static electricity inside the tube to help make the picture. **Power stations** use static electricity to remove pollution particles from their exhaust smoke. Static electricity is also used to apply the toner to the drum of a photocopier. (*See also:* **Current electricity** and **Van de Graaf generator**.)

▶ **Static, static electricity** – Static attraction can be demonstrated by rubbing balloons on a sweater. They will then stay in place as if by magic.

Stove

In an electric stove **electricity** is changed into heat **energy** and used to cook food.

The electric stove was invented by St. George Lane-Fox in England in 1879. He designed electrical **heating wires** that were insulated from their surroundings (*see:* **Insulator**), which are called a heating **element**. This design is still used today.

The top of the stove usually has four spiral heating elements. There are other wires in an element that provide heat in the walls of the oven and the grill.

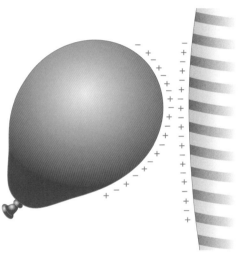

▲▼ **Static, static electricity** – How charges build up on the surface of a balloon. Before rubbing (above) and after rubbing (below).

▼ **Stove** – Electric stoves have hot plates with either elements or halogen lamps inside them to produce rapid and controllable heat.

Substation

A place where very high-**voltage electricity** from a **power station** is changed into lower-voltage electricity for use in homes, schools and factories.

Electricity is transported from power plants along **cables**. They may be carried overhead by **pylons** (**transmission lines**) or buried in the ground. In the cables the electricity is at a high voltage so that it can be moved easily over long distances. This high voltage is too dangerous for people to use; so when the cables reach a town, the electricity is converted to lower voltages at the substation.

Electricity at the lower voltage is sent along smaller cables to all the consumers in a neighbourhood.

Switch

A device for breaking the flow of **electricity** in a **circuit**. It allows you to control the flow of electricity. Switches are found on most electrical equipment, for example, **radios** and **flashlights**.

A switch contains two plates that can be brought together or pushed apart. These **contacts** have to be quite strong because, as the contact is made or broken, a **spark** jumps between them. The spark can melt a little part of the surfaces of the contacts. Over time, the contacts in a switch are burned out.

Usually, at least one of the contacts is made of a springy metal. To make a contact, the switch lever is pushed down on the springy contact, thus completing the circuit. When the lever is turned to the off position, the lever pressure is removed, and the contact springs apart again.

Different kinds of switches are used for low-**voltage** and **household power supplies**. You can safely touch low-voltage supplies, so you can even make a switch out of two paper-clips that swivel on drawing-pins. However, in the case of household supplies, a much greater amount of protection is needed, and the switch contacts are placed behind thick plastic covers (*see:* **Plug** and **Socket**). (*See also:* **Dimmer switch**.)

Contact
Contact

◀ **Switch** – A simple rocker switch of the kind used in low-voltage circuits uses a rocker to make and break the contacts. One contact is made of springy metal. The switch is off unless the switch rocker is pushing the contacts closed. A modified version of this switch is used in household lighting systems.

▼ **Switch** – The rotary switch, as found on the volume knobs of radios, for example, uses a cam (a lump on a disc) to lift the springy contact and break the circuit.

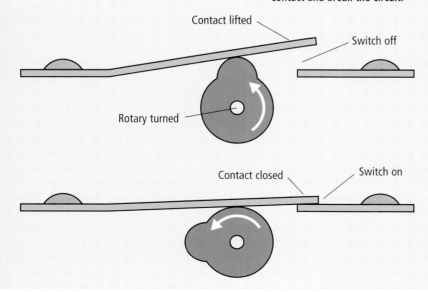

Contact lifted
Switch off
Rotary turned
Contact closed
Switch on

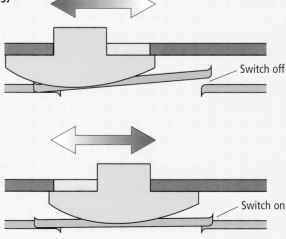

Switch off
Switch on

▲ **Switch** – A slider switch contains a metal strip that moves with the slider. This kind of switch is found on flashlights.

Symbols

An electrician's shorthand for each of the **components** in a **circuit**. (*See also:* **Battery** and **Series Circuit**.)

T

Telegraph

The earliest form of fast electric communications. It used a very simple **circuit** consisting of a **power** source (in the form of **accumulators**) connected through a **switch** to a **meter** or to a device that punched holes in a paper tape. The switch was used to send messages.

The important feature was that the receiving device could be a long way away from the transmitting switch.

A number of different devices were used to help transfer messages more efficiently. The one that came into general use was a coding system developed by Samuel Morse, called Morse Code.

A paper tape-recording of the first historic message transmitted in 1844 by Samuel F. B. Morse

read, when decoded, 'What hath God wrought?' It was sent by him from the Supreme Court room in the Capitol to his assistant, Alfred Vail, in Baltimore.

Television

A piece of electrical equipment designed to convert radio waves into pictures and sound. The messages to make the pictures and sounds are carried on radio waves between the television studio and the television set. Large numbers of complicated **circuits** are used in television cameras and television sets.

The first television camera and television set were invented by John Logie Baird in 1926. Since then many changes have been made to produce the television cameras and sets we use today.

The view from a television studio that you see on your television set is made in this way: a camera in the studio takes in light and changes the **energy** in the light rays to **electricity**.

A microphone in the studio takes in sound and changes the energy in sound into electricity too. The electrical signals are then

converted to radio waves at the transmitter. The radio waves travel through the air from the transmitter. If you have your television set switched on, the radio waves that strike your television **antenna** generate electrical **currents**. They travel through the circuits in your set and are converted back into sound and light.

Cable TV is a relatively new development that allows electrical signals to move directly to the television through **cables** and removes the need for an antenna. It also reduces interference and improves the quality of the signal.

(*See also:* **Amplify**; **Cathode-ray tube**; **Coaxial cable**; **Coil**; **Static, static electricity**.)

Tesla, Nikola

A Serbian–American (1856–1943) who discovered how to produce **alternating current (AC)**.

Thermistor

A **semi-conductor** that changes its **resistance** markedly with temperature. They are also called temperature-sensitive **resistors**. They can be used as electrical thermometers.

▼ **Telegraph** – This diagram shows the principle of the telegraph.

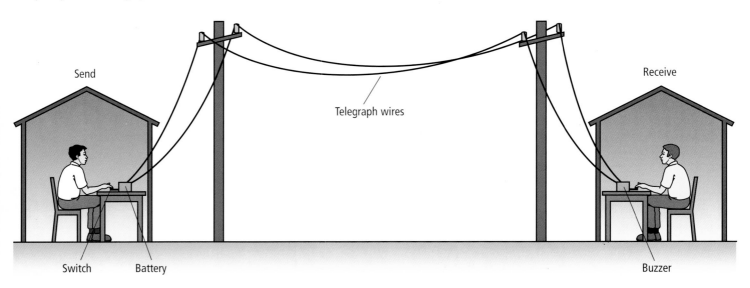

Send

Telegraph wires

Receive

Switch   Battery

Buzzer

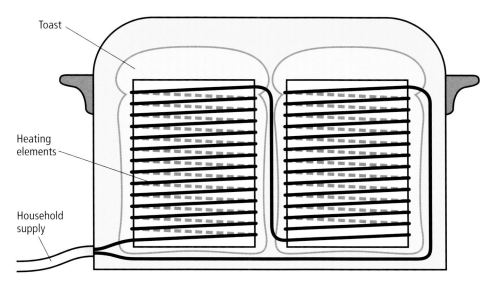

Toast

Heating
elements

Household
supply

▲ **Toaster** – This diagram shows the pattern
of the heating elements.

Transistor

A miniature **semi-conductor**
invented by William **Shockley**
and co-workers in 1947. Like
a **vacuum tube**, a transistor
regulates **current** or **voltage** and
acts as a **switch** or **amplifier** for
electronic signals.

A transistor is made of a
'sandwich' of three layers of semi-
conductor material. Each layer is
capable of carrying a current.
The central layer of the sandwich
controls the flow of **electricity** just
as a grid does in a vacuum tube.

Toaster

An **appliance** with two sets of
heating elements in-between
which you place a slice of bread.
When you switch on the toaster,
electricity flows through the
elements, and the **wires** get hot,
heating the surface of the bread.

The first toaster was invented
by the General Electric Company
in the United States. It went on sale
in the shops in 1913. This toaster
could only toast one side of bread
at a time. In 1923 another toaster
was invented that turned
the bread around to toast
both sides. Finally, in
1927 the pop-up toaster
was invented. When
you put the bread in
this toaster, you set
off a heat-activated
switch. When the
toast is ready, the
device unfastens a
catch, and the bread
pops up.

Transformer

A device for changing the **voltage**
of an AC (**alternating current**)
electricity supply.

It is mainly used to step down
the very high voltage carried by
transmission lines to the lower
voltage needed for home use (*see:*
Household electricity).

A transformer consists of two
coils of **wire** wound around a
common loop of iron. The

alternating flow of electricity in
one coil (the primary) causes,
or induces, electricity to flow
in the other (secondary) coil. If
the primary coil contains more
windings than the secondary coil,
then the electricity flowing in
the secondary coil will have a
lower **voltage**, and vice versa.
Transformers can thus be used to
step up as well as step down.

▼ **Transformer** – A transformer consists
of paired coils on a common iron core.

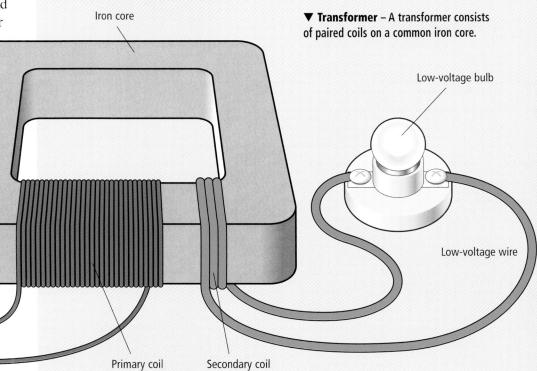

Iron core

High-voltage AC
power supply

Primary coil   Secondary coil

Low-voltage bulb

Low-voltage wire

Transmission lines

Large **cables** designed to carry very high-**voltage electricity** from a **power station** to where it is needed. Transmission lines are supported on metal frames called **pylons**. (*See also:* **Electricity grid**.)

U

Utility poles

Wooden, metal, or reinforced concrete poles used to carry local **power** lines in a city. (*See also:* **Electricity grid**.)

V

Vacuum tube

A device, once common in electronic **circuits**, designed to control the flow of **electricity**. Its main uses were to make the **current** flow in only one direction (a **rectifier**) or to **amplify** a **voltage**. Vacuum tubes were a vital part of the development of electronics and were used in the first **radios**, **televisions** and computers, but they have been virtually obsolete for many years.

A vacuum tube has a heater contained inside a glass bulb (often tubular in shape). An electric current flows through the heater, and **electrons** are attracted from it to another electrode (called an anode). The flow of electrons, and thus of electric current, can be controlled by placing a perforated metal sheet between the heater and the anode. The vacuum tube is controlled by altering the voltage on the perforated metal sheet (called a grid).

Vacuum tubes are bulky and need a large amount of electricity to run the heaters. They were never suited to portable equipment,

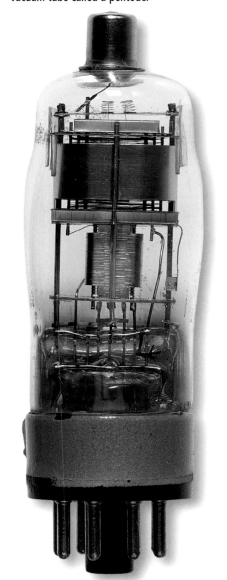

▼ **Vacuum tube** – This is a type of amplifying vacuum tube called a pentode.

and the age of portable electronic devices such as radios was only possible once the **transistor** had replaced the vacuum tube. (*See also:* **Cathode-ray tube**; **Edison, Thomas Alva**; **Semi-conductor**.)

Van de Graaff generator

A mechanical **generator** for producing **static electricity**. A rapidly revolving **motor** makes a belt turn rapidly; and as it brushes against a sphere, static electricity builds up on the surface of the sphere.

Variable resistor

A **resistor** whose value can be changed. Also known as a **potentiometer**. Variable resistors are made of a material that has a relatively high **resistance**, such as carbon. One end of the resistor is connected to a **circuit**, and the arm that slides over the resistor completes the circuit. When the arm is at one end of the resistor,

▼ **Van de Graaf generator** – The generator produces enough voltage to make hairs on this person's head develop enough of the same charge to repel one another. That is what makes the hairs stand on end.

the resistance is low; but when the arm is at the other end, the resistance is high. The volume control on a **radio** is a common type of variable resistor. (**Dimmer switches** on household lighting do not use variable resistors because the heat generated would cause a danger of fire.)

Volt (V)
The unit of measuring **voltage**. It is named after Alessandro **Volta**, a pioneer of **electricity**.

Volta, Alessandro
An Italian pioneering scientist (1745–1827) who, in 1800, made the world's first **battery**, based on the earlier discovery of Luigi **Galvani**. Volta's battery was called the voltaic pile because it was actually a pile of **cells**. The unit for measuring **voltage**, the **volt**, is named after him. (*See also:* **Electricity and its history**.)

Voltage
The electrical 'pressure' that a **battery** or other source of **electricity** can provide. Voltage is measured in **volts** (abbreviated to V) after Alessandro **Volta**. A single **dry cell** normally provides 1.5V; a **household electricity** supply provides 240V.

If you increase the voltage, you increase the electrical pressure in the **circuit**. For example, if you put two 1.5V dry cells end to end, the voltage of each **cell** is added together, so the result is a 3V battery. This battery will make a **light bulb** shine more brightly than if only one dry cell (and therefore 1.5V of pressure) were used.

Power stations generate very high-voltage electricity (*see:* **Generator**). The high pressure allows them to send very large amounts of **electric power** along

relatively thin **transmission lines** in a very efficient way. However, very high voltages cannot be used in the home, so the voltages are stepped down by **transformers**. (*See also:* **Ohm's Law**.)

Voltmeter
A **circuit tester** set up to measure **voltage**.

W

Wall socket
(*See:* **Socket**.)

Watt (W)
The unit of **electrical power**. One thousand watts equal one **kilowatt**. Most electrical devices are rated in watts. For example, **light bulbs** are sold as 25W, 100W and so on. (*See also:* **Watt, James**.)

Watt, James
A British engineer and scientist (1736–1819), who was responsible for many important advancements

in steam power. James Watt lived before the era of **electricity**. However, the unit of **power** is called the **watt** in honour of his achievements.

Wind generator, wind power
A method of converting the power of the wind into **electrical power**. The blades of a wind turbine are connected to the shaft of a **generator**, so that, when the blades turn, **electricity** is produced by the generator. Sites with frequently windy conditions, such as coastal locations or hilltops, are needed to reliably operate a wind generator. Wind generators are environmentally friendly in that they do not burn **fossil fuels**, but they are unsightly and can spoil the look of the landscape.

Wire
A strand or strands of metal designed to be thin enough to be flexible. Wires are used to connect **components** in a **circuit**.
(*See also:* **Conductor** and **Flex**.)

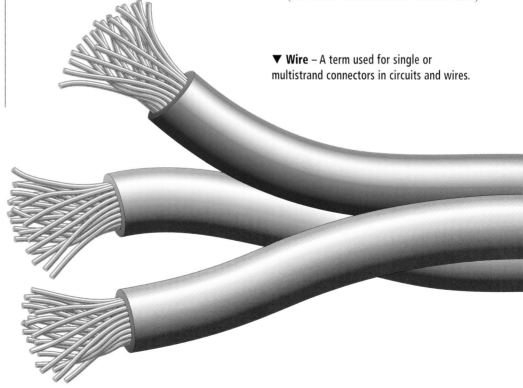

▼ Wire – A term used for single or multistrand connectors in circuits and wires.

Index

μF (see: **Capacitor**)

A
AC (see: **Alternating current**)
Accumulator 3
Adapter 3
Aerial (see: **Antenna**)
Alkaline battery 3
Alternating current (AC) 3
AM 4
Amber (see: **Electricity and its history**)
Ammeter 4
Amp (A) 4
Ampere (see: **Amp**)
Ampere, André Marie 4
Amplify 4
Amplitude modulated (see: **AM**)
Antenna 4
Appliance 4–5
Arc light 5
Armoured cable 6
Attractive force 6

B
Bar magnet (see: **Magnet**)
Battery 6–7
Bayonet fitting (see: **Light bulb**)
Bell, electromagnetic 7
Blackout 8
Brownout 8
Bulb (see: **Light bulb**)
Buzzer 8

C
Cable 8
Capacitor 8
Car battery (see: **Accumulator; Battery; Negative terminal; Positive terminal; Secondary battery, cell**)
Carbon (see: **Conductor; Dry cell; Resistance; Resistor; Variable resistor**)
Cathode-ray tube 8–9
Cell 9
Charge 9
Chemical energy (see: **Battery**)
Chip (see: **Silicon chip**)
Circuit 9–10
Circuit board 10
Circuit breaker 10–11
Circuit diagram 11
Circuit tester 11
Coaxial cable 11
Coil 11
Compass 12
Component 12
Conductor 12–13
Contacts 13
Conventional current (see: **Electricity and its history; Electron**)
Cooker (see: **Stove**)
Copper (see: **Conductor; Resistance**)
Coulomb (C) 13
Current 13
Current electricity 13

D
DC (see: **Direct current**)
Dielectric 13
Dimmer switch 13
Diode 13
Direct current (DC) 14
Dry cell 14
Dynamo 14

E
Earth (see: **Ground**)
Economy battery (see: **Battery; Dry cell; Primary battery, cell**)
Edison Screw fitting (see: **Light bulb**)
Edison, Thomas Alva 14–15
Electric heating (see: **Heating, electric**)
Electrical energy 15
Electric generator (see: **Generator**)
Electricity 15
Electricity and its history 15–16
Electricity grid 16
Electricity supply (see: **Household electricity; Power supply**)
Electric power 16
Electric power generator (see: **Generator**)
Electric shock 16
Electrolysis 16–17
Electrolyte 17
Electromagnet 17
Electromagnetic field 17
Electron 18
Electron gun (see: **Cathode-ray tube**)
Electroplating 18
Element, electrical 18
Element, heating (see: **Element, electrical**)
Energy 18
Energy-saving light (see: **Fluorescent light**)

F
Farad (F) 18
Faraday, Michael 18
Filament 18
Flashlight 18–19
Fleming, J.A. (see: **Edison, Thomas Alva**)
Flex 18
Fluorescent light 20
FM 20
Force 20
Fossil fuels 20
Franklin, Benjamin 20
Frequency modulation (see: **FM**)
Fuse 20–21

G
Galvani, Luigi 20
Galvanometer (see: **Ampere, André Marie**)
Generator 20–22
Geothermal power 22
Gray, Stephen (see: **Electricity and its history**)
Grid (see: **Electricity grid**)
Ground 22

H
Halogen lamp 22
Heating, electric 23
Heating element (see: **Element, electrical**)
Henry, Joseph (see: **Generator**)
Hertz, Heinrich Rudolf (see: **Photoelectric cell**)
History of batteries (see: **Battery**)
History of electricity (see: **Electricity and its history**)

Horseshoe magnet (see: **Magnet**)
Hot wire (see: **Live wire**)
Household electricity 24–25
Hydroelectric power 25

I
IC (see: **Integrated circuit**)
Immersion heater 25
Incandescent 26
Induction 26
Insulator 26
Integrated circuit 26
Iron 26

J
Junction of wires 26

K
Kilowatt (kW) 26

L
Lamp (see: **Halogen lamp; Light bulb**)
Lane-Fox, St George (see: **Stove**)
Lead–acid battery (see: **Battery**)
Leyden jar 26–27
Light bulb 27
Light-emitting diode (LED) 28
Lighting (see: **Arc light; Edison, Thomas Alva; Fluorescent light; Halogen lamp; Light bulb; Photoelectric cell**)
Lightning 28
Lithium battery (see: **Battery**)
Live wire 28
Load 28
Lodestone (see: **Magnet**)

M
Magnet 29
Magnetic field 30
Magnetic pole 30
Magnetism 30
Magnetite (see: **Magnet**)
Metals (see: **Conductors**)
Meter 30
Microchip (see: **Integrated circuit**)
Morse, Samuel F. B. (see: **Telegraph**)
Motor, electric 31
Multimeter (see: **Circuit tester**)
Musschenbroek, Pieter (see: **Electricity and its history**)

N
Negative terminal 32
Neon lighting 32
Neutral wire 32
Nichrome (see: **Conductor; Heating, electric; Resistor**)
North pole 32

O
Ohm 32
Ohm, Georg Simon 32
Ohmmeter 32
Ohm's Law 32–33
Ørsted (O) 33
Ørsted, Hans Christian 33
Overload 33

P
Parallel circuit 33
Pentode (see: **Vacuum tube**)

Permanent magnet (see: **Magnet**)
Photocopier (see: **Electricity; Static, static electricity**)
Photoelectric cell 34
Photovoltaic cell 34
Piezoelectricity 34
Plug, electrical 34–35
Pole 35
Positive terminal 35
Potentiometer 35
Power 36
Power-generating station 36
Power grid (see: **Electricity grid**)
Power station (see: **Power-generating station**)
Power supply 37
Primary battery, cell 37
Pylons 37

Q
Quartz watch/clock (see: **Piezoelectricity**)

R
Radio 38
Radio waves (see: **Antenna; Radio**)
Rechargeable battery, cell 38
Rectifier 38
Remote control (see: **Electromagnet**)
Repulsive force 38
Resistance 38
Resistor 38
Rheostat 38

S
Secondary battery, cell 38
Semiconductor 39
Series circuit 39–40
Shock (see: **Electric shock**)
Shockley, William B. 40
Short circuit 40
Silicon (see: **Semiconductor; Silicon chip**)
Silicon chip 40
Socket 40
Solar cell (see: **Diode; Photovoltaic cell**)
Solar farm (see: **Solar power**)
Solar power 40
Solenoid 41
South pole 41
Spark 41
Static, static electricity 42
Stove 42–43
Street lighting (see: **Edison, Thomas Alva; Fluorescent light**)
Substation 43
Supply (see: **Power supply**)
Suppressor (see: **Static, static electricity**)
Switch 43
Symbols 44

T
Telegraph 44
Telephone (see: **Electromagnet**)
Television 44
Temperature-sensitive resistor (see: **Thermistor**)
Tesla, Nikola 44
Thermistor 44
Thermostat (see: **Heating, electric; Iron**)
Toaster 45
Torch (see: **Flashlight**)
Transformer 45

Transistor 45
Transmission lines 46
Tungsten (see: **Conductor; Filament; Light bulb**)
Tuning coil (see: **Coil**)

U
Utility grid (see: **Electricity grid**)
Utility poles 46

V
Vacuum tube 46
Valve (see: **Vacuum tube**)
Van de Graaff generator 46
Variable resistor 46–47
Volt (V) 47
Volta, Alessandro 47
Voltage 47
Voltaic pile (see: **Volta, Alessandro**)
Voltmeter 47

W
Wall socket (see: **Socket**)
Watson, William (see: **Electricity and its history**)
Watt (W) 47
Watt, James 47
Wet cell (see: **Accumulator; Battery**)
Wind generator, wind power 47
Wire 47
Wirewound resistor (see: **Resistor**)

Z
Zinc–carbon battery (see: **Battery**)